PHOTOGRAPHY AND
THE OLD WEST

1.   John C. H. Grabill, "VILLA OF BRULE." 1891

PHOTOGRAPHY AND THE OLD WEST

Text by Karen Current

Photographs selected and printed by
William R. Current

Published by Harry N. Abrams, Inc.,
in association with the Amon Carter Museum of Western Art

The Amon Carter Museum was established in 1961 under the will of the late Amon G. Carter for the study and documentation of westering North America. The program of the museum, expressed in publications, exhibitions, and permanent collections, reflects many aspects of American culture, both historic and contemporary.

This project is supported by a grant from the National Endowment for the Arts in Washington, D.C., a Federal agency.

Editors: Margaret L. Kaplan, Ellen Shultz
Designer: Deborah Jay

Library of Congress Cataloging in Publication Data

Current, Karen.
    Photography and the Old West.

    Bibliography: p.
    1. Photography—The West—History.   2. Photographers
    —The West—Biography.   I. Current, William.   II. Title.
TR23.6.C87   779'.9'978   77-27857
ISBN 0-8109-1412-3
Library of Congress Card Catalog Number: 77-27857

Published in 1978 by Harry N. Abrams, Incorporated, New York

Printed by Morgan Press, Inc., Dobbs Ferry, N.Y., in Quadradot Lithography
Binding by Publishers Book Bindery, Long Island City, N.Y.

Editors' note to the plates: The editors have attempted faithfully to reproduce the photographer's title or inscription when known. However, spellings and punctuation have been modernized. For location and ownership of individual photographs see page 272.

Contents

DEDICATION

To those intrepid photographers . . .
Who faced the unknown,
*   sometimes at great peril,*
*   often with no knowledge to guide them in their empirical art,*
*   and with materials and equipment unsure;*
Who braved hazards and physical hardship
*   too frequently dying poor and forgotten*
*   but for those moments of time they worked so hard to preserve;*
Who paid, often, an enormous personal price
*   to leave imprints of reality (that we can know in no other way);*
*   images in silver, though slowly fading, to preserve our heritage.*

We salute you.

PREFACE

This collection of photographs of the West is unique, for it has been selected from the viewpoint of William R. Current, who is himself a photographer and artist. *Photography and the Old West* was conceived and organized by him as a series of one-man shows, to convey as nearly as possible what a few of the many early photographers hoped to express in their work. There are no "anonymous" images—cameras, not people, make anonymous pictures.

The text also reflects much of William Current's thoughts and insights, formulated over many years in the course of his own commitment to photography as an art form. He contributed greatly to the writer's understanding of how people learned to use a camera and became camera-wise in an individual way, and how tools and materials affected a photographer's seeing, as well as to the realization of the impact and importance of the visual document.

K. C.

ACKNOWLEDGMENTS

Anyone who has compiled research and has written a manuscript for publication understands the multiple meanings behind the simple word "acknowledgments." The people who become involved throughout the course of a book's life—whether in a professional, personal, or peripheral capacity—and who help to bring it into being, are many and indispensable. Their contributions are invisible among the pages, yet they are an inextricable part of the book's form and content.

We must begin by acknowledging the Amon Carter Museum and The National Endowment for the Arts which, together, provided a matching grant to produce this publication and the traveling exhibition of photographs. Mitchell A. Wilder, the museum's director, who gave us that important initial encouragement when he first heard the idea, deserves special recognition.

Our exploration of the photography of the West commenced at the Henry E. Huntington Memorial Library. Gary Kurutz, now library director at the California Historical Society in San Francisco, started us on our quest, and we are indebted to him for his patient searches, invaluable suggestions, and interest in the study. His successor, Alan Jutze, proved equally helpful. Carey Bliss approved the use of the Huntington's collections and aided us in many ways, even to his wry comments. The professional staff of the Huntington Library was also most helpful and knowledgable, and to each of them we owe special thanks.

Several photographic historians provided invaluable insights and information. We are especially grateful for conversations with Richard Rudisill of the Museum of New Mexico, and the late Terry Mangan.

Professional librarians provided us with assistance and information far beyond the scope of their paid tasks. Kenneth I. Pettitt, head librarian of the California Section, California State Library, and Joan Hofmann of the Beinecke Rare Book and Manuscript Library, Yale University, deserve particular mention. Jack Haley at the University of Oklahoma contributed valuable information about Oklahoma history as we studied the photographs. Tina Wilkinson, great-great granddaughter (and forthcoming biographer) of the photographer Frederick I. Monsen, generously opened her files to us. Miss Julia C. Watkins, the ninety-four-year-old daughter of pioneer Carleton E. Watkins, shared unforgettable remembrances of her father and his colleagues, among them John Muir and William Keith.

Numerous friends contributed significantly to the progress of this work. Among photographers, the late Wynn Bullock deserves special mention: he viewed each group of photographs carefully, considered the concepts thoughtfully, criticized gently and constructively, and, as in everything he undertook in photography and art, brought fresh enthusiasm to the project. We miss you very much, Wynn.

Many people substantially aided us in researching, collecting, and copying photographs in their collections. Without them, the exhibition would have been impossible. We thank the staffs of the California State Library, the State Historical Society of Colorado, and the Albert Bender Rare Book Room at the Stanford University Library for allowing the photographer to set up his equipment and make negatives directly from the prints. Sincere appreciation is extended, too, to the many staff members who gave every effort to making first-quality negatives from their photographs, on the understanding that they would be used for exhibition purposes; the historical societies of Arizona, Nebraska, and Utah; The Denver Public Library; the University of Oklahoma; the Southwest Museum; the Beinecke Rare Book and Manuscript Library at Yale; and again, the Henry E. Huntington Library.

Three individuals who privately own collections made these available to us, and were very helpful: Glenn E. Miller, Rell G. Francis, and Jack Coffin.

Many institutions contributed to the research and overall understanding of the subject, though their collections are not represented in the exhibition. The Museum of New Mexico; the Austin Public Library and the Fort Concho Museum in Texas; the Forestry Library of the University of California at Berkeley; and the state historical societies of California, Kansas, Montana, and South Dakota all made their resources available to us. We are very grateful to the staffs of these archives of historical materials.

The United States Geological Survey in Denver preserves with great care early photographs from the explorations. The Library of Congress and the Smithsonian National Anthropological Archives have riches that we only touched upon superficially. Each of these institutions, as well as the National Archives, provided us with invaluable research materials.

Karen Current
William R. Current
Pasadena, 1978

INTRODUCTION

Photography is, simply put, a record fixed on silver of the radiation (or light waves) reflected or emanating from objects. Our eyes, like the camera, collect the rays, but they can fix them only in memory. Photography has its own reality: unlike painting, photographic image-making exists without man. A camera can record images while orbiting in space or scan a building from a preset position, capturing in minute detail all within its field of view. Such images become indisputable eyewitness accounts of an event such as a bank robbery, or of a place as remote as Mars. The informational content is real and trustworthy.

Yet the camera itself is only a tool. It cannot distinguish the meaningless from the momentous; it merely intercepts and records. It is the photographer, working behind the camera, who determines the artistic possibilities. John Moran, brother of the painter Thomas Moran and himself a photographer, observed in 1865 that "in the actual production of the work, the artist ceases, and the laws of nature take his place. But it is the power of seeing and deciding what shall be done, on which will depend the value and importance of any work, whether canvas or negative."[1]

This work is an explanation of the role of the nineteenth-century photographer as a conscious historian of the West—a recorder of events, people, and places as surely as were the diary-keepers, journalists, and writers. Like them, he exercised choice in what he recorded; unlike them, he documented aspects of reality that we can know in no other way. A photographer's technical ability may often have been slight, his composition awkward, his total statement less than eloquent, but early photographs, like the work of writers, artists, and toolmakers, are part of the historical narrative. They may be the best —and are sometimes the only—record we have.

Photographers as documenters are too often casually, even carelessly, regarded. Historians who meticulously cite the sources of important facts freely use photographs while omitting the name of the photographer even when it is known. A recently televised historical series carefully attributed sayings and writings to those quoted while flashing photographs without a mention of their makers.

Photographs as irreplaceable documents, too, have been badly treated. Diligent record-keepers have meticulously saved the most trivial notes, believing they might contribute to the larger picture of a moment, while discarding the pictures themselves. The United States Copyright Office, recipient of untold numbers of photographs, for years threw them away when the copyright expired. Millions of prosaic words have been preserved while photographs were judged solely on the interest or usefulness of their subject matter. One choice collection was culled for photographs relevant to a particular place and the remainder "ditched." Another photographer's life's work was copied on microfilm and the plates were discarded.

Paradoxically, many early photographers have been dredged from obscurity in recent years, and invested with artistic values and aesthetic considerations that thrust them into the mainstream of American art. Such judgments rarely bear relationship to the photographer's own ideas or intent in preserving a particular moment. The lunar silence of Timothy O'Sullivan's stark sand dunes or the glacial isolation of Carleton E. Watkins's Yosemite can suggest an aesthetic to modern man unknown to the photographer and perhaps more profound, but to evaluate photographs responsibly the ideas of the photographer, insofar as they can be determined, the purpose for which he made his image, and the equipment available to him must be assessed.

To the early expeditionary or survey camera man, the primary purpose was to record an event and a place with as much skill and interest as possible. Other early photographers sought to startle with images of places few had seen. While viewers today judge how well and inventively the medium of photography itself is utilized, apart from the imagery presented, early photographers were far more concerned with content. (An exception, of course, was Eadweard Muybridge and his studies of animals in motion.)

Style could almost be defined as the manner in which a photographer overcame the extreme limitations of process and equipment, yet diversity existed among the field photographers. Definable stylistic characteristics are not always evident in every picture, but the body of work produced by many of the pioneer photographers reveals a camera-wise sense, an individual way of seeing, and clarity of vision. John Hillers's ordering of architectural forms, O'Sullivan's feeling for contour, Watkins's sense of placement are stylistic elements that distinguish their work.

It is difficult—and useless in many cases—to evaluate photographers by their prints. Old prints have suffered from use, abuse, and neglect, only recently becoming valued as collectables. Photographic materials have often degenerated, and ignorance of preservation techniques has contributed to the loss of uncounted photographs. Some notable works have survived in pristine condition, however, and these are extremely valuable as a measure of photographic print quality.

By today's standards, printing was a mechanical rather than a decision-making process. Printing-out paper had little latitude or possibility for manipulation. Many of the survey prints were issued by indifferent galleries or government laboratories, which in O'Sullivan's case scratched and rescratched numbers on the plates. Many early photographers produced stereographs, or negatives for graphic translation by artists. As John Towler lamented, it was not unusual for a photographer to "run all sorts of risk, make every effort, incur immense expenses in order to secure first-rate negatives, and then frequently abandon the gem into the hands of an indifferent assistant, which is tantamount in many instances to leaving the negative to print itself."[2]

A century of experience has changed the way we regard photographs. For many contemporary viewers the print is an art object quite apart from the thing seen; the photograph of a century ago was appreciated largely for its informational content or entertainment value. Photographers such as Watkins and Muybridge, who made fine prints as objects, enjoyed a brief period of success but turned to books or portfolios, binding series of prints in oversize albums. Photographs as objects could not compete in the highly decorative interiors of the period. The detail and subtlety of tonalities died in red plush.

Photography and the Old West is intended to convey as clearly as possible how people learned to use a camera and became camera-wise in an individual way; how tools and materials affected photographic seeing; and what a few of the many early photographers hoped to express. The photographs have been chosen by William R. Current, a photographer and artist, whose own subject matter is the West. He has stood where many of those early image-makers stood and has evaluated the photographs from several viewpoints. The chosen works exist on all levels, as do works of prose or paintings, and they are open to a wide range of interpretation. That is the ambiguity—and beauty—of photography.

This work is not a comprehensive survey but rather a selective look at some of the imagery of the West that a few conscious photographers produced. It is only a beginning.

NOTES

1. John Moran, "The Relation of Photography to the Fine Arts," *Philadelphia Photographer* 2 (1865): 33.

2. John Towler, *The Silver Sunbeam*, 4th ed. (New York: J. H. Ladd, 1865), p. 182. This is the best manual on collodion photography. Professor Towler was editor of *Humphrey's Journal of the Daguerreotype and Photographic Arts*.

2. William Henry Jackson, NEAR SAPINERO, ENTRANCE TO THE BLACK CANYON, DETAIL

Photography and the West

Photography and the West came of age in post-Civil War America. Photography moved from the studio to the field, and the West emerged as a vast, rich resource for scientific and scenic exploration. Both offered a new frontier to master, and each exerted an immense magnetism on the war-weary American mind. For the scientist the West presented a vast laboratory where new data could be gathered and old questions, superficially formulated, answered; to the photographer the West loomed as a great visual unknown. Together they shared the pioneer experience, and for the first time in history the exploration and discovery of a new land were witnessed and recorded with the camera.

Photographers sought to photograph the land almost as soon as its image could be fixed; thus, the history of expeditionary photography is almost as old as photography itself. Among the first attempts on the North American continent were those of the intrepid Frederick Catherwood and John L. Stephens, who made daguerreotypes as well as drawings on their 1841 expedition into the Yucatán.[1] Unfortunately, no daguerreotypes from this expedition seem to have survived.

Colonel John Frémont made the first attempt to capture the West on silver on his initial expedition. He met with the group's scorn and little success.[2] In 1851 the daguerreotypist W. C. Mayhew accompanied Captain Lorenzo Sitgreaves's expedition along the Zuni and Little Colorado rivers; some of his work has been pub-

lished recently.[3] Two adventurers succeeded in 1853 in capturing expeditionary images with the daguerreotype process: Solomon Carvalho with Colonel Frémont's expedition through the San Juan Mountains, and John Mix Stanley on Governor I. I. Stevens's railway survey. From Carvalho's account of his experiences, one marvels at his perseverance and success under nearly impossible conditions: "Buffing and coating plates, and mercurializing them, on the summit of the Rocky Mountains, standing at times up to one's middle in snow," in temperatures ranging "from freezing point to thirty degrees below zero."[4] But daguerreotypy simply proved too slow, too difficult, and too expensive for such work.

With the advent of collodion and the stereographic camera, making possible much faster exposures at far less cost, more expeditionary photography was attempted. In 1857 Lieutenant Joseph Ives casually remarked, "There being a little photographic apparatus along, I have taken advantage of the mild and quiet interval to experiment." Had he succeeded in photographing his voyage up the Colorado River to the Black Canyon, he could have claimed the honor—and probably not inconsiderable profits—of making the first images of the Grand Canyon. But almost immediately the wind blew both tent and apparatus away, and the lieutenant dismissed his photographic effort as "comparatively of little importance."[5]

Other attempts followed. In 1859 Captain J. H.

Simpson took two photographers along to record his expedition into the Great Basin of Utah. Evidently they made only stereographic views—and those none too well. The captain was disappointed not only by the poor quality, but because the stereo was "not adapted to distant scenery."[6]

Albert Bierstadt, the artist, accompanied Captain Frederick W. Lander's party on its survey from Puget Sound to South Pass. He produced both sketches and a set of stereo views which later proved highly useful as reference for many of his Rocky Mountain paintings. In 1859, also, a photographer named J. D. Hutton traveled with Captain William F. Raynolds's expedition, but little is known of the photographic effort. With that, expeditions and expeditionary photography came to a halt.

Before the Civil War, few photographers ventured into the western wilderness to photograph on their own; expense was an obstacle, but the surprising fact is that, with rare exceptions, no one conceived that vast expanse of land as subject matter. None of the early photographers who emigrated West and opened studios on the frontier in the 1850s seems to have taken photographs en route (Peter Britt traveled to Oregon in 1852 and Charles R. Savage to Salt Lake in 1860; Joseph Buchtel appeared in Portland in 1853 and George Wakely in Denver in 1859). During the 1860s, too, they seldom attempted anything but portraits.[7] The only photographers who ventured into the land, most notably Savage, Carleton E. Watkins, and Charles L. Weed, did so from well-established portrait studios in the older settlements, Salt Lake City and San Francisco.

In the East, however, the uses of photography grew. The government "found it of vast importance during the war," as the work of such photographers as Captain Andrew J. Russell and Alexander Gardner proved.[8] The war induced numerous professionals to leave their sun-roofed galleries and studios for the cold light of the battlefield. Mathew Brady privately financed teams of photographers, training more as the war progressed, until he reportedly had twenty-two separate units in the field.

The difficulties were many, the dangers formidable. "Instantaneous" photography, in terms of the collodion process, meant several seconds, and the equipment presented a large and conspicuous target. "The battle of Bull Run would have been photographed 'close up' but for the fact that a shell from one of the rebel field-pieces took away the photographer's camera," reported O'Sullivan.[9] But from that arena the camera emerged as a battle-tested instrument. Prior to the war Captain Simpson wrote, "In my judgment, the camera is not adapted to explorations in the field," concluding that "the cause lies in some degree in the difficulty, in the field, at short notice of having the preparations perfect enough to insure good pictures."[10] War technologies had improved the preparations and spurred their production. And in addition they had forged a new breed of photographer, thoroughly professional and tempered in extreme conditions.

The West, too, emerged from the sixties with a new facade. As people averted their eyes from the painful memories of war, the American West filled their vision. "The new sense of the land was scientific and realistic;

it was chiefly the work of a handful of naturalists, geographers, and landscape planners."[11] Clarence King, a young man with very large ideas, embodied the new vision. To him the West presented itself as an uncharted geological laboratory where his "religious, esthetic and intellectual interests" could find room to conduct "an earnest and loving study of God's work of nature."[12] King, among the first graduates of the Sheffield School of Science at Yale, had been a protégé of Professor William Brewer, working with him on the State Geological Survey of California, a model of its kind. At twenty-five, he qualified as a seasoned veteran of geological field study.

Prior to the war, explorations belonged almost exclusively within the province of the military. Culling enormous amounts of data of varying usefulness from the records of sundry expeditions, a young man named Gouverneur Warren made a comprehensive map which delineated with amazing accuracy the shape and contour of the regions west of the Mississippi River. Now the scientists sought to fill in the details.

In 1866 the young King proposed an incredibly ambitious survey "to examine and describe the geological structure, geographical condition and natural resources" of a one-hundred-mile-wide strip of land, stretching from the California Sierras to the border of Nebraska, an immense area.[13] To accomplish his self-appointed task he gathered a team of highly educated young scientists of particular expertise, and he hired the specialist in field photography, Timothy O'Sullivan. Professor Brewer may have suggested it. "On our trip, in 1863, I talked

much about the value of large photographs in geological surveys. . . . In later years King was the first to carry out these ideas on a grand scale; and now the camera is an indispensable part of the apparatus of field work in such surveys."[14]

With King, photography and the West entered a new phase of exploration and discovery. Used as a piece of scientific apparatus, the camera made particular readings of the topography, depicting the lay of the land as well as the textures and formations of the geological structures within it. The camera instantly documented a place and the natural and environmental relationships that existed there, while years might pass before the volumes of scientific data emerged.

The photographer as team member added another dimension to the survey—he chronicled the event itself. Stories of exploration and travel, credible as they might be, did not carry the impact or believability of the photographic witness. Wilderness explorers and mountain men such as Bill Williams and Lewis and Clark had hacked and tracked great paths into the unknown, but their feats of daring could only be imagined. The new explorers, while documenting the substance and detail of the land, could show proof of the exploration and the adventure itself. Thousands of descriptive words had and would be written, but the camera provided actuality.

The impact produced by the photographic image—incredibly convincing, often sensational—can hardly be overestimated. Neither Ferdinand Vandiveer Hayden nor Major John Wesley Powell had hired a photographer to accompany him on his respective explorations in

1869, but they did so from that date, as did Lieutenant George M. Wheeler. "Competition between the Great Surveys made the inclusion of this novel means of advertising a virtual necessity which was not overlooked."[15]

At the same time, private businessmen saw the potential of the photograph as a means of advertisement and publicity for their western endeavors. The railroad took Captain A. J. Russell aboard to chronicle both the momentous event of tying two oceans together and the picturesque aspects of the land. Spilling ties and rails across the land from the cornucopia of Congressional bounty, the railroad magnates sought to feed the dream visually with photographic evidence that the transcontinental railroad was akin to the long-sought Northwest Passage or the magic route to India.

Full-plate photography in the postwar West demanded a large amount of capital, a means of transport, a good deal of stamina, and no small measure of patience. The tools of the craft and the means of transporting them were costly; the equipment, bulky, fragile, and heavy; and the limitations of photographic technology bound all photographers to the time exposure. It was the wet-plate collodion process that made field photography possible.

Collodion had been developed barely a decade after the invention of daguerreotypy, and it was this process that nearly all the early photographers in the West used, with the exception of Philadelphia photographer William Bell, who used tannin dry plates on the 1872 Wheeler expedition. The discovery of collodion as a vehicle for light-sensitive salts had revolutionized the medium of photography; the increased difficulty of process was more than compensated for by the dimensions it added to both the kind and nature of the image.

From the direct positive that was reversed from left to right in a daguerreotype, collodion produced a negative, latent image that could be righted in the print. In contrast to the falsified tones of the daguerreotype image on silver that could be viewed only in reflected light, halftones emerged on the paper print from the collodion negative. The expensive one-of-a-kind daguerreotypic image was challenged by relatively inexpensive paper copies from one negative, and while the daguerreotype rendered detail, collodion duplicated it with extreme delicacy. The daguerreotype emerged from the camera as an unalterable whole; the sun-print could be manipulated to a limited extent in the printing-out process and the paper print cropped. Finally, the most important advantage came from the lessened exposure time of collodion over daguerreotypy, though it by no means made instantaneous photography possible.

From guncotton and hens' eggs came the stuff of the new process, collodion and albumen. In 1846 C. F. Schonbein invented a process for making guncotton, intending to use it as an explosive agent in firearms.[16] Like many discoveries, the material came to have important applications in entirely unrelated fields. The medical profession immediately found several uses for the membranous material when it was discovered that guncotton colloids (or gelatinizes) in sulphuric ether to form a sticky, gelatinous substance that adheres when the ether evaporates. Frederick Scott Archer saw that the transparent, colorless skin would make an excellent vehicle in which to suspend light-sensitive silver salts for potential photographic images. Collodion, when applied to glass, sensitized with silver, and exposed and developed before drying, allowed the silver salts to arrange themselves into an image. Archer had the prescription for the wet-plate process that dominated image-making for the next thirty years; although easier methods had been devised, none could equal its speed. With that, collodion spread over the next three decades onto everything from glass to sheet iron. Any mechanically adept, slightly adventurous chemist could set up his darkroom-laboratory and try his hand at the "black art."[17] Thousands did. One can scarcely overstate the attraction photography held. The number of professional photographers jumped from less than one thousand in the 1850s to over three thousand in the 1860s.[18]

Collodion moved photography from the realm of the remarkable to the plebeian. As a portrait business, photography flourished at every level. Almost everyone could afford to have some kind of portrait made. While professional photographers in studios turned out the new "social currency"—photographs the size of calling cards called cartes de visite—like newly minted money, itinerant practitioners began to produce tintypes in all sizes.[19]

Collodion having paved the photographic path from the glass house to the outdoors, enthusiastic amateurs moved onto the land to make stereographic views. "There is no branch of photography that has so intensely attracted the attention of wealthy and intelligent amateurs as that of stereography."[20] Equipped with a small camera having a short focal-length lens, or a stereo camera fitted with a pair of lenses, a reasonably sharp image could be obtained with the aperture wide open. One did not have to know much artistically to end up with an interesting view. One simply sought a scene with a definite object in the foreground (to render a sense of distance), and the resulting realism compensated for poor composition and picture defects. While stereos have a stage-set quality, with the fore-, middle-, and background compressed, the scene hovers in space when magnified and rendered three-dimensional through the stereopticon viewer. The magic feeling that it is not just a picture of a place, but the place itself, is undeniably enchanting. The effect produced, for the amount of care expended, placed the stereograph in the realm of the marvelous. From a three-by-seven-inch negative, thousands of stereos could be reproduced on a correspondingly small piece of photographic paper. Nearly everyone could afford his own picture gallery, and a person could be transported beyond the solitude and isolation of an Ohio farm to the wonders of the world. The rise in popularity of the three-dimensional photograph was meteoric because of collodion, and the number of stereographs that made faraway places a province of American sitting rooms is rightly guessed to be in the millions. The firm of E. and H. T. Anthony placed an order for ten thousand stereos with William H. Jackson alone, for his views made along the railroad in 1869.[21]

In December, 1863, *The Silver Sunbeam*, Professor John Towler's comprehensive manual on the collodion process, appeared. Within a year it went into a fourth edition of one thousand copies. In the preface the publisher declared, "There are some twelve or fifteen thousand Photographers in the United States, each one of whom ought to possess the book"[22] (his estimate may have been a bit generous).

Although prepared collodion and other chemicals became commercially available during the war, Professor Towler explained in complete detail the processes involved in the preparation of every material in the photographer's arsenal, from guncotton to cutting one's glass. Photographers, particularly those in the West, used as many commercial products as possible—the process itself was complicated and cumbersome enough. Simplified, the procedure for preparing and exposing a collodion wet plate in the field went something like this:[23]

Clean the glass. To a flawless piece of glass, apply a cleaning compound such as decomposed limestone. Add a few drops of alcohol and rub with Canton flannel, keeping fingers off surface. Remove other particles with sable or camel hair brush.

Coat the plate. Pour prepared collodion evenly over glass until thoroughly coated. William H. Jackson's son described watching his father perform this operation: "The process of preparing a wet-plate and developing it called for great skill and art. I recall, as a small boy, seeing my father coat an 18×22 plate. He balanced it carefully on the thumb and fingers of his left hand, poured a pool of collodion in the far, left-hand corner of the plate, and then slowly worked the thick fluid about the edges and all over the plate until it reached the near,

right-hand corner. So sure and careful was his hand that never a drop was spilled, nor was there any fluid left to be returned to the collodion bottle. This was hard enough to do in the studio, let alone on the top of a mountain in driving gales, after packing cameras, plates and plate-holders up over ledges slippery with ice and across treacherous fields of snow."[24]

Sensitize the plate. When collodion is set but tacky (ether and alcohol having evaporated), immerse plate in vertical bath of silver nitrate. This reacts to form silver bromide and silver iodide from the bromides and iodides of the metals in prepared collodion. They in turn form nitrates in solution. Wait up to five minutes and drain the plate.

Expose the plate. Slip damp plate into holder and expose plate while wet, up to ten minutes. Remove the still-wet plate in its holder to a dark area.

Develop the plate. Remove plate from holder in dark tent and flow the developing solution evenly over the plate, using the same method as for spreading collodion. Silver deposits group where light has penetrated to the plate.

Rinse the plate. Rinse both sides of plate thoroughly in water. (In field photography, finding and carrying a water supply was a major consideration.)

Fix the image. Free image from salts that temporarily supported it by immersing in solvent of silver iodide until the image, composed of reduced silver, is permanently fixed. If negative is thin or weak, the image can be intensified to increase shadows and middle tones.

Rinse the plate. Rinse plate well to rid of chemicals,

using clean water supply. Keep water in motion if possible.

Dry the plate. Dry carefully by passing over lamp flame.

Varnish the plate. While the plate is still warm, protect the emulsion by flowing with varnish.

To protect the plate from actinic action until the image was fixed, a dark tent had to be found or erected in the field. Thus, the space in which to perform these chemistries was usually minimal and the danger to health frightful.

Field photography required almost equal amounts of ingenuity and equipment. The latter included:

View camera. The camera itself approximated a piece of furniture, constructed and joined of heavy wood. Likewise, the tripods, plateholders, and slides were fabricated of solid wooden pieces. The larger the camera, the heavier the entire outfit.

In large view cameras, such as Carleton Watkins's 18-by-22-inch camera, the distance from front to back—lens to plate—extended more than three feet. It was extremely cumbersome to use. Several adjustments requiring dexterity and speed had to be made at both ends of the camera before each exposure. After an exposure, the photographer hurried to his dark tent to develop his still-wet plate; therefore, photographers tried to work within a few feet of it, as evidenced by the appearance of a dark tent in so many early pictures. It was not always possible, however, and at Tower Falls in Yellowstone William Henry Jackson set an endurance record: "To get any comprehensive view of the falls, it was necessary to go to the bottom of the ravine below, a descent of about two hundred feet, through steep sides covered with a thick growth of small timber and brush. Rather than take the dark box down to the bottom, I worked from the top. Backing my plate with wet blotting paper, and wrapping the holder in a wet towel and the dark cloth, I scrambled and slid down to the rocky bed of the stream, with plate holder and camera in hand. After taking the picture, I had a slow, laborious climb back again, and reached the top out of breath in a wringing perspiration. Four round trips gave me the desired number of negatives, a full day's work, making a stiff price in labor for the one subject."[25]

Ground glass. Viewing a scene through the dull ground glass involved educated guesswork. With small aperture lenses, very little light struck the ground glass, and therefore illumination fell next to zero at the edge. In addition, ground glass corners were cut away on a diagonal to allow air to escape from the bellows, so composing to the edges approached artful approximation at best.

Lenses. The best lenses available to photographers came largely from two competitors, John Henry Dallmeyer of England and C. C. Harrison, designer of the American-made Globe Lens. Both lenses took in an extremely wide field of over seventy degrees and, though not designated as such then, the focal length of each was about seventeen inches. Each offered minor differences and advantages; both were expensive.

None of the early lenses was fully color-corrected to diffract the light rays of the spectrum, as fine modern lenses are. By the same token, the collodion process could not register the full visual spectrum, and these limitations compensated each other. Collodion registered overly sensitive in the blue range of the spectrum and barely so in the red, but with the heavy blue reflectance from the sky bathing the landscape, the resulting image had an overall range of tonality, though somewhat distorted. Skies inevitably blanked out from overexposure if the photographer exposed for the elements of the landscape, which disturbed many. Still, outdoor subject matter did not have the same crucial requirement for tonal truth as did the human face.

The flare factor was a familiar phenomenon to field photographers. Extraneous light entering the lens caused internal reflections both in the lens and bounding off the bellows onto the plate. In some cases the resulting flare may have improved a collodion exposure, for it tended to heighten the shadows, but it also degraded the tone in the light areas and cut sharpness considerably.

Shutters. The length of exposure—at the very least ten seconds, and increasing with the size of the plate—precluded the need for a shutter mechanism.[26] Photographers simply uncapped their lenses to expose the plate.

Glass plates. A photographer calculated the number of plates he carried according to the time he expected to stay in the field, and his mistakes never returned with him. He cleaned the plate and reused it. Encased in a holder, the glass negative (for the large view camera) was as unwieldy as a casement window. Obviously, glass of any size and quantity accounted for hefty poundage, but that created less difficulty for the photographer than did the fragility of the plates and containers. The sheer number of times the glass had to be handled accounted for most of his field disasters. A cracked plate was impervious to the best retoucher's brush; a broken one worthless.

Dark Tent. When he journeyed into the field, the photographer of necessity invented or transported a dark place in which to coat and develop his plates. Some photographers mounted a portable tent upon a tripod, a black contraption just large enough to fit over the head and with just enough space to manipulate the plates. Others rigged a movable wagon, and the clever improvised in the field. Frederick Monsen described one such tent in the desert: "I very well remember my improvised dark tent in Death Valley, the hottest desert in the world. I dug a hole in the sand, spread my tripod over it, and covered it with blankets, until it was perfectly light-proof—as well as hermetically sealed from the air. Then, stripping to the buff, I crawled into the hole, and used the rim as a table. It was effective enough, but a trifle tropical. I labeled this invention 'The Photographic Dark Tent and Turkish Bath Combined,' and would be pleased to send specifications to anyone who is still a devotee of medieval methods."[27]

Transport. A variety of inventive means of transport came into use in the West, the photographer resembling everything from a hearse driver to an itinerant showman. Carleton Watkins packed twelve mules with his equipment into Yosemite; a wagon rig served well in some areas; Timothy O'Sullivan outfitted a Civil War-type ambulance. Inevitably the photographer resorted to brawn at some point. Hillers's river scenes and Jackson's high mountains depended upon strong backs.

Thus equipped with the tools and chemicals of the trade, a photographer's trappings weighed hundreds of pounds. On the surveys, however, nearly every photographer had the benefit of assistants or experienced packers, and though packing and unpacking could be tiresome, a photographer could pack a day's supply and go through the entire image-making process in one-half hour. Both men and mules grumbled over carrying the equipment, and sometimes the packing was so careless that photographers suspected sabotage. Perhaps the most remarkable fact is that so many glass images survived.

Beyond the mechanical, the photographer contended with the weather. Like farmers and fliers, photographers from the earliest days were weather-watchers, and the wind was ever the adversary. The *Philadelphia Photographer* warned, "The wind is . . . a real foe to the photographer, when he is afield, and wishes to make sharp negatives of foliage and shrubbery. A gentle puff of air mixes up his tree tops and flexile branches in a most distressing manner. . . . Few but photographers know how really rare a breezeless day is."[28] Equipment often blew over or away. The elements imperiled not only photography but health. Hillers reportedly turned blue from the cold and O'Sullivan collapsed in 120-degree Death Valley heat. Bugs and illness harassed them constantly. Hillers nearly died from a scorpion's bite.

To make a clean negative, an essential of fine photography, was not easy in the field. Static electricity in dry atmosphere wreaked havoc with glass, attracting dust and specks like a magnet; a muddy river sometimes supplied the only water available.

Photographers learned to read their negatives in the field, judging them on the basis of whether they were printable within certain limits rather than on the fineness of a potential print. Printing waited for a more permanent setup during winter months, or else the negatives were sent to commercial galleries or to government laboratories.

Printmaking depended upon sunlight, quantities of print frames, and plenty of time. Photographers almost without exception preferred albumenized paper because the smooth, glossy surface best rendered the sharpness of detail and the tonal range that collodion negatives produced. Professor Towler explained in minute detail how to prepare one's own paper, but quantities were commercially available. Oliver Wendell Holmes reported that the Anthonys' concern alone had an army of ten thousand hens to produce enough albumen-laden eggs for paper.[29]

The process for making prints from the matrix of the negative involved a series of unalterable steps, with its own formula and pace, more than selective judgments on the part of the photographer. The printer proceeded as follows:

Sensitize the paper. Just before use, sensitize the already albumenized paper by floating the sheet in a solution consisting of silver nitrate, citric acid, alcohol, and water. Let it remain about five minutes. Hang to dry.

Load the print frame. Place the glass negative, collodion-side upward, in the frame, and the albumen paper, sensitized-side downward, together. Ideally, a soft cloth or Canton flannel as buffer between the paper and print-frame back should be used. Lock the double doors of the back. Place frame in sunlight.

Print-out the negative. Expose in sunlight and check progress of printing-out from time to time in a shaded corner, to determine development of contrast. Printing-out paper allowed little latitude for manipulation, the process itself imposing its own restraints. Once the forms began to darken areas of the paper, they became self-masking, blocking further penetration by light with their own contrast. Thus blocked, dark areas and shadows never printed to dead black and the print could be exposed for maximum highlight, while the middle areas had a chance to build. To a degree, the printing-out paper compensated for the overexposure collodion required. A watchful printer could render a fairly long tonal scale in the final print.

Stop the actinic action. Unload the print frame in a darkened room illumined only by subdued yellow light. Rinse prints, keeping them in motion in a water bath for up to five minutes. Remove to a second and third bath, repeating the process for five minutes for each bath.

Toning. Before toning, pass prints through a hot water bath, then immerse in toning solution, usually gold chloride. When gold has reacted with some of the silver in the image and replaced it to the desired degree (purplish brown to purplish black), remove the prints and again wash in hot water.

Fix the print. Fix the image in either cyanide of potassium or hyposulphite of soda, performing this step under yellow light until fixing is complete. Remove the print from the solution and immerse in water.

Rinsing. After draining the print, rinse for several hours in clean water to remove all fixer. Turn and move frequently.

Printmaking, too, involved health hazards. Dr. Towler recommended cyanide of potassium over hyposulphite of soda to fix positives, suggesting it could also be used to remove black stains caused by silver nitrate. He cautioned, "Another trouble . . . arises from the mode we practice of turning the prints round with the hands in the toning and fixing baths. The health of operators is much impaired, and especially in those large printing establishments, where a number of females are employed in this department, who, by this continual manipulation in the two fluids, are frequently in a suffering condition."[30] He suggested the use of glass rods, but that did not eliminate the exposure to the chemicals.

Enlarging. The solar camera, a very expensive device which resembled a reflecting telescope, constituted the only form of enlarger. The camera turned on an equatorial mount in order to place it in a direct line with the moving rays of the sun. With this device a photographer could either reduce or enlarge the size of the negative image, but printing by this method required a long exposure in strong light, with the resulting sharpness less than the original.

The American mind, with its Yankee penchant for gadgetry and inventiveness, took to photography immediately. Inventive tinkerers, the mechanically minded, the how-to-do-it man, dabbled incessantly with the medium. Given the complication and mess of wet-plate chemistry in combination with the heavy equipment, collodion photography fell under male dominance, with women's involvement in the black art largely limited to commercial gallery work or cleaning up.[31]

Photography manifested the same frontier appeal as the West. Both seemed to be within the reach of anyone, and the common man felt sure that he could conquer both, given a little practice and the exercise of his ingenuity. Photography was a new frontier.

NOTES

1. "The results were not sufficiently perfect to suit his [Catherwood's] ideas. . . . They gave a general idea of the character of the buildings, but would not do to put into the hands of the engraver," recorded Stephens. It is remarkable that Catherwood had any success, given the difficult tropical conditions. From John L. Stephens, *Incidents of Travel in Yucatan*, 2 vols. (1843; reprint ed., New York: Dover Publications, Inc., 1963), 1:100.

2. Richard Rudisill, *Mirror Image* (Albuquerque: University of New Mexico Press, 1971), pp. 101–2.

3. Lorenzo Sitgreaves, "Report of an Expedition down the Zuni and Colorado Rivers," 32nd Cong., 2nd Sess., *Sen. Exec. Doc. 59* (1853), gives no mention of Mayhew among the party. He may have been in the area of Santo Domingo, where the party assembled and from where it departed in August, 1851. Though they are dated 1850, the Mayhew photographs were first published in Weston J. Naef in collaboration with James N. Wood, *Era of Exploration: The Rise of Landscape Photography in the American West, 1860–1885* (Boston: New York Graphic Society, 1975).

4. Solomon Carvalho, *Incidents of Travel and Adventure in the Far West* (New York: Derby & Jackson, 1857), pp. 20–21. Copies were made at Mathew Brady's gallery and the images used in Frémont's memoirs, but the precious originals apparently perished in fire. See Walt Wheelock, "Frémont's Lost Plates," *Westerner's Brand Book, San Diego Corral* 2 (1971): 48–53.

5. Joseph C. Ives, "Report upon the Colorado River of the West," 36th Cong., 1st Sess., *H. R. Exec. Doc. 90* (1861), p. 32.

6. James H. Simpson in *Report of Explorations Across the Great Basin of the Territory of Utah in 1859* (Washington, D.C.: Government Printing Office, 1876), p. 8.

7. Robert Taft, *Photography and the American Scene* (New York: Macmillan Co., 1938), p. 269.

8. *Philadelphia Photographer* 3 (1866): 170.

9. John Samson, "Photographs from the High Rockies," *Harper's New Monthly Magazine* 39 (1869): 465.

10. Simpson, *Report of Explorations*, pp. 8–9.

11. Lewis Mumford, *The Brown Decades* (1931; reprint ed., New York: Dover Publications, Inc., 1955), p. 65.

12. Thurman Wilkins, *Clarence King* (New York: Macmillan Co., 1958), pp. 44–45.

13. Gen. A. A. Humphreys to King, 21 March 1867, Fortieth Parallel Survey Records, RG 57, National Archives, Washington, D.C.

14. Brewer, quoted in The Century Association, *Clarence King Memoirs* (New York: G. P. Putnam's Sons, 1904), pp. 323–24. In addition, the publication issued by the California Geological Survey in 1865, of which King had been a member, contained photographic prints of Yosemite by Carleton Watkins.

15. In his treatment of the western explorations, William H.

Goetzmann is among the first to recognize the importance of the visual image, both in enhancing and verifying the scientific data of the great surveys. William H. Goetzmann, *Exploration and Empire* (New York: Alfred A. Knopf, 1966), p. 437.

16. Helmut Gernsheim in collaboration with Alison Gernsheim, *History of Photography* (London: Oxford University Press, 1955), p. 153. Unfortunately guncotton burned too fast and was extremely dangerous.

17. This designation was first given photography by Oliver Wendell Holmes, who advised, "Cover your hands in gauntlets of India Rubber, if you would not utter Lady Macbeth's soliloque [*sic*] over them when they come to the light of day." "Doings of the Sunbeam," *Atlantic Monthly* 12 (1863): 4.

18. Taft, *Photography*, p. 61.

19. Holmes wrote that tintypes were available for as little as two cents each, or, "a dozen chefs d'oeuvre for a quarter of a dollar." "Doings," p. 3.

20. John Towler, *The Silver Sunbeam*, 4th ed. (New York: J. H. Ladd, 1865), p. 66.

21. Beaumont Newhall and Diana E. Edkins, *William H. Jackson* (Dobbs Ferry, N.Y.: Morgan & Morgan, Inc., 1974), p. 137.

22. Towler, *Silver Sunbeam*, p. iv.

23. Technical information has been taken from the literature of the day and from L. P. Clerc, *Photography: Theory and Practice*, 3rd ed. rev. (London: Sir Isaac Pitman & Sons, Ltd., 1954), still one of the most comprehensive textbooks on photographic chemistry and techniques.

24. Clarence S. Jackson, *Picture Maker of the Old West, William H. Jackson* (New York: Charles Scribner's Sons, 1947), p. vi.

25. William Henry Jackson and Howard R. Driggs, *The Pioneer Photographer* (Yonkers, N.Y.: World Book Co., 1929), p. 112.

26. A table of exposure times for the various photographic processes gives useful comparisons. See Gernsheim, *History of Photography*, p. 377.

27. Frederick I. Monsen, *With a Kodak in the Land of the Navajo* (Rochester, N.Y.: Eastman Kodak Co., n.d.), p. 22.

28. *Philadelphia Photographer* 2 (1865): 19.

29. Holmes, "Doings," p. 2.

30. *Silver Sunbeam*, p. 222.

31. One woman complained of silver stains and acid holes in the linen, her best porcelain dishes ruined with photographic use, the stink of chemicals in the house, and her china closet expropriated for photographic purposes. "It has just occurred to us why so many amateur photographers are bachelors. The reasons are obvious, after reading this paper," responded the unsympathetic editor Edward Wilson, *Philadelphia Photographer* 2 (1865): 57–60.

CARLETON E. WATKINS
(1829–1916)

In 1849 Carleton E. Watkins sailed for San Francisco—where he would find a career, and spend most of his life—with his friend Collis P. Huntington, a man of enormous ambition and sharp business sense. Thus began the western venture of a would-be photographer and his lifelong friend.

How Carleton Watkins became a photographer is an oft-quoted story, but the experience of finding himself thrust into the profession by chance and fortune was not atypical. He had neither artistic training nor background, nor had he ever made a photograph when the successful daguerreotypist Robert Vance asked him to replace temporarily the daguerrean operator in Vance's San Jose gallery; but Carleton gamely hopped a stage to San Jose to act as caretaker until an operator could be hired. When Vance visited him the next week, without having found a replacement, he gave Watkins a few basic instructions and suggested that he bluff his way through the Sunday portrait sittings. The following week an operator could re-do the pictures if necessary.

But Watkins paid attention and read the few books then available on daguerreotypy; he became the daguerrean operator. Vance had found both an able and competent man for his gallery and a lifetime profession for Watkins, who proved to be more than suited by nature and talent for photography.

Watkins, an affable and outgoing person, initially enjoyed the portrait business. He stayed in the San Jose gallery for several years, occasionally traveling about to photograph. He made a short trip in 1856 to the New Almaden Quicksilver Mine to photograph the mining operations, and he may have journeyed as far as the Mariposa Grove in 1859. His name appeared in the San Francisco directory in 1861 as a daguerrean operator. In that year, as the guns of Fort Sumter signaled thousands to the battlefield, Watkins ventured into the interior of California, embarking upon the first of countless journeys to photograph the already famous Yosemite.[1]

For his first venture, an 18-by-22-inch camera had been constructed to his specifications. The idea of using such a heroically scaled apparatus probably derived in part from the grandness of scale of the subject itself, and in part from the availability of the new wide-field Globe Lens which encompassed 75 degrees. With it he would make the largest outdoor views taken in California up to that time.[2]

To reach the "Grizzly Bear" in Yosemite was a feat in itself; once there Watkins needed a caravan to transport his equipment: "At least twelve mules were required to pack the outfit of the indomitable photographer . . . the tent used in coating and developing these plates was a load for one mule. This young man was compelled to take five mules in his train carrying camera, tent, etc., around the Valley with him, from point to point."[3] Tech-

3.   FILLING IN SECRET TOWN TRESTLE. C. P. R. R.

nically the images from this excursion would not measure up to the quality that Watkins soon achieved and for which his work became distinguished, but from this initial endeavor evolved a lifelong pursuit of the grand view. His talent and love for outdoor photography began to outgrow the confines of a portrait studio. He continued to make portraits and cartes de visite, but he also traveled to Yosemite as often as possible, for as long as feasible, to make his grand views. Commercially, the market for such views in that culture-hungry, affluent city made this possible, and the quality of his work justified the extraordinary effort required. Oliver Wendell Holmes wrote of the photographs in 1863: "As specimens of art they are admirable, and some of the subjects are among the most interesting to be found in the whole realm of Nature. Thus, the great tree, the 'Grizzly Giant,' of Mariposa, is shown in two admirable views; the mighty precipice of El Capitan, more than three thousand feet in height—the three conical hill-tops of Yo Semite, taken, not as they soar into the atmosphere, but as they are reflected in the calm waters below—these and others are shown, clear, yet soft, vigorous, in the foreground, delicately distinct in the distance, in a perfection of art which compares with the finest European work."[4]

The name Watkins soon became synonymous with Yosemite. His views found their way to influential senators when the draft for the Yosemite Act was submitted, and purportedly to the desk of President Abraham Lincoln when the bill reached him for signature in June, 1864. Once Yosemite officially became the first area to be preserved for the people by Congress, Frederick Law Olmsted commissioned Watkins and two painters, Virgil Williams and Thomas Hill, to make individual studies of the park scenery and to advise him on how the beauty of the park might be preserved and enhanced for the enjoyment of Americans.[5]

In 1865 Professor J. D. Whitney published his first volume of the *Geological Survey of California*, offering "to make the peculiar features of the Yosemite more intelligible to those who have not seen it, or who have not enjoyed, what is next best to the thing itself, the admirable photographs of Mr. C. E. Watkins." He further noted, "They are already well known and widely distributed through the Eastern States."[6]

Obviously successful, Watkins became the proprietor of a large establishment appropriately titled the Yosemite Art Gallery. While photographs of the Yosemite region predominated, they were by no means his only offerings. As early as 1865 Watkins photographed the Mendocino Coast (datable by the structures)[7] and, of course, he took scenic views around the San Francisco and Bay areas. A notoriously poor record-keeper, Watkins's whereabouts are difficult to place during those years.

He continually returned to the Yosemite region for months at a time. In 1866 he encountered part of the California Survey party, among them Clarence King and James Gardner. Professor Whitney took advantage of Watkins's presence and asked him to make a set of pictures; in 1868 Whitney incorporated the images in *The Yosemite Book*. That same year brought further international recognition to Carleton Watkins. His Yosemite views won the acclaim of the judges at the Paris Exposition Universelle and first prize for photographic landscape.

Watkins worked hard to obtain his views, not only to wield his huge camera and plates but to find a place to stand. The ethnologist and historian William DeWitt Alexander described following "a trail on a ledge [Sunnyside bench] in the face of a precipice some 600 feet high. We had some ticklish spots to cross where a stumble or a slip might have been fatal," only to find at the end of their arduous climb that "Mr. Watkins had his photographic apparatus up here and took pictures at the foot of the fall."[8]

Watkins liked traveling companions, but when he photographed he worked alone. He developed his own methods and techniques, but his ideas for equipment had to be fabricated by others since he himself was not adept with tools. He was admired by other photographers, among them Charles R. Savage, who wrote to the *Philadelphia Photographer*:

> Among the most advanced in the photographic art, none stands higher than Mr. E. C. Watkins [*sic*], who has produced, with his camera, results second to none in either the eastern or western hemispheres. I spent many pleasant hours with him, and found him ever ready to communicate information to the ardent photographer.
>
> I was somewhat curious to learn his *modus operandi* for producing his large views in a climate so dry and difficult to work in. After so much attention to photographic ware, porcelain, rubber, and other material, for making baths, I found *his* to consist of pine wood coated heavily with shellac. In addition to this, he uses the water bath, by means of which he can take a greater number of pictures without losing his chances while the light is good. His negatives are taken, developed, and then placed in the water bath until he is ready to finish them. Just think of carrying such huge baths, glasses, etc. on mule back, and you can form some idea of the difficulties in the way of producing such magnificent results.[9]

The Watkins gallery prospered and the camera man broadened his travels, leaving the operation of the gallery to assistants. In 1868 he made his first trip to Oregon to take both stereo and large views. Undoubtedly he was not the first photographer to see Oregon's scenic wonders, for a number of photographers early inhabited the Northwest, but his photographs were the first of such size and distribution. B. P. Avery commented on Watkins's "splendid series of large views in the Yosemite Valley. A new series along the Columbia River, recently taken, is equally fine."[10] Watkins produced flawless negatives and equally faultless prints, the skies without a fleck or mar, and even in tone.[11]

In 1870 Clarence King re-entered Carleton Watkins's life, having received an order to continue exploration. Timothy O'Sullivan was unavailable, so King engaged Watkins as photographer. The explorations centered on the inactive volcano chain along the Pacific Coast, and for this assignment Watkins used the same format, approximately 8-by-12 inches, as O'Sullivan. Like his predecessor, Watkins went far beyond the commission, though the images, again, were intended for scientific purposes. His views from Mount Shasta and Mount Lassen are extraordinary high-mountain images.

In 1872 the Yosemite Art Gallery expanded. Described as luxurious and elegant, the walls were lined with 18-by-22-inch prints framed in black walnut, a gilt band edging the matted photographs, "not only miracles of photographic art, [but] delineations of the finest residences and views to be found in San Francisco."[12] The writers warned, however, of exorbitant prices (in 1867 Watkins advertised his portfolio of Yosemite views for one hundred and fifty dollars).

Together with the artist William Keith, Watkins traveled to Utah. Watkins had an annual railway pass, courtesy of his railway-magnate friend Collis Huntington, in return for which he performed photographic services gratis. The photographer and artist left for their three-month trip late in 1873.

Ironically, the essence of Watkins's livelihood—scenic views—both created and destroyed his gallery within the next few years. To photograph he had to leave the gallery and business; in doing so he invited the ruin that ultimately arrived. Watkins was as negligent and careless in business matters as his friend Huntington was shrewd, and during one of his photographic jaunts his studio and its contents were auctioned to satisfy financial obligations he had neglected. The photographer I. W. Taber acquired the lot and had no scruples in selling his former colleague's work with the Taber stamp on it.[13]

Watkins was as hurt by the betrayal as by the financial reverse. He immediately set out to recover his losses, rephotographing views which sold well and distinguishing them from previous work with the label "Watkins' New Series." Yosemite remained a favored subject, though competition had begun to make inroads into that market, and he sought new material. His intuitive eye explored the subtle relationships between the man-made and nature, and he reached a maturity evident in a variety of grand panoramas. He traveled to Virginia City, and in that bleak scape he took a sizable number of views of the mines and the city. He began to photograph the mission chain in California at a time when each mission lay suspended between an encroaching civilization that threatened its territory and the natural order that sought to return the structures to the land. Watkins sometimes waited as long as two weeks at one mission for a perfect light.

In early 1880, at Collis Huntington's behest, Watkins traveled along the line of the Southern Pacific Railroad to the end of the track and on to Tombstone. His large views of Casa Grande and the mission of San Xavier del Bac, like those of the other missions, are valuable historical documents as well as fine photographs of high technical quality. One wonders how he managed a spotless giant negative. "It has been blowing sand night and day," he wrote, and "it is so hot and dry that it is very difficult to work the chemicals."[14] He photographed the trains, roundhouses, and scenery along the line, and from these negatives he compiled a large portfolio, bound into a handsome album for Huntington. It is possibly the only set of these views that exists.[15]

Watkins's New Series revealed the photographer's uncanny talent as a producer. He was a master at staging groups of people within his compositions. He knew exactly what he wanted, and his extroverted, easy manner with people made it possible to create his perfectly placed, carefully posed groupings. "Filling in Secret Town Trestle," "Waiting for the Train," and the view of the roundhouse, with crew and Indians casually yet attentively posed, are masterfully composed.

The decade of the eighties was a shaky one financially. Watkins "was always generous to a fault, but more of an artist than a business man. . . . He made enormous amounts of money from this photographic work, but through friends lost it all."[16] The photographer was still optimistic, however. The rich and influential remained his clients, commissioning Watkins to photograph their sumptuous mansions and ordering custom-made albums of his original prints. For several clients he produced one-of-a-kind folio albums comprised of grand views of a patron's estate—interior, exterior, and grounds. Gilt-edged and elegantly bound by hand, these albums can hardly be lifted by a single person.[17]

The decade of the 1890s brought many changes to both photography and the photographer. It heralded not only the age of the Kodak but the era of the half-tone process, which put the photograph into print. No longer was a photograph a unique and sought-after item, but Watkins became too ill, and perhaps too old, to change. The beginning of the new century found the photographer almost totally blind and destitute, but he apparently realized the historical importance of his early images.

Rather than sell them for commercial purposes,[18] he began to negotiate with Stanford University to serve as a repository for his life's work. The 1906 San Francisco earthquake and fire destroyed that hope. His life's labor ended in ashes. So did his will. Watkins abandoned the city that he had loved and photographed for most of fifty years, moving to the eighty-acre ranch in the Sacramento Valley that his old friend Collis Huntington had deeded to him.

If any one of the early photographers can be said to represent the collodion era, it is Carleton Eugene Watkins. He came of age with field photography, and he was one of its earliest and best practitioners. He remains a master of the "Grand View." He knew what the large format could express and he exploited its potential fully. He did not seek the part that characterized the whole; he attempted to capture the whole itself. Rarely does one find close-ups or medium-distance views. It is the grandness, regardless of subject, that he intuitively saw, and in its expression that he excelled.

There is a complexity to his seeing. Not everyone could attempt such grand views. Watkins's photographs are so skillfully composed that the scale and organization of picture planes appear natural, the roads and trails leading lines rather than intrusions into the composition. Every element adds to the whole—there is no clutter of unrelated objects—and he composed to the edge, no mean accomplishment in a large format.

His technique was impeccable. Wielding his enormous camera and plates, with correspondingly large lenses and accouterments, Watkins consistently produced meticulous negatives and immaculate prints. To maintain an even quality in such an ungainly size, particularly out in the open, magnifies our sense of wonder both for the man and the way he used the medium.

Watkins's photographs of Yosemite were the first grand views that established and documented a natural wonder in the West. He photographed the noted features that became the landmarks by which Yosemite was known all over the world, and his continued trips to the region yielded more and more aspects of that scenic wonder as it became accessible. All of his views render a sense of place, as seen by a highly competent image-maker. If his pictures seem familiar and common to viewers today, perhaps it is because many are the prototypes for countless views that have followed, and the place itself, with its colossal grandeur and unique features, suggests its own viewpoints. His photographs were highly acclaimed in both American and European circles for their artistry. E. L. Wilson, editor of *Philadelphia Photographer*, wrote: "Every one has doubtless heard of the magnificent scene of the Yosemite Valley. . . . Who shall not say that in *this* instance, at least, the *camera is mightier than the pen.*"[19]

Watkins's photographs provide not only a benchmark in several wilderness areas, as do O'Sullivan's and Jackson's, but they are also arrested moments in the dynamics of man's westward intrusions on the landscape. He imagized its multiple manifestations—the towns, mines, transportation, and architecture—in grand views that are extremely important historical documents.

Above all, Watkins was a producer.

His talent in creating a picture by directing and arranging people within it was uncanny. In his intuitive placements and careful groupings, the figures do more than simply scale his scenes; they achieve compositional and tonal force. Under his direction, people seem aware and emotionally in tune with the picture. There is a vitality in their bearing that suggests that they are part of the picture, not simply in it; they humanize and counterpoint the man-made. They evoke an emotional response one scarcely feels with any other early work, and more skillful arrangements have rarely been found in pictures since. It took considerable personality and persuasion to produce such arresting, lively pictures, particularly in the days of time exposure.

NOTES

1. *Bulletin of the New York Public Library* 56 (1952): 375. Watkins was not the first picture-maker in the area; one of Vance's partners, Charles L. Weed, had preceded him in 1859 and had returned with stereos and some larger views (10-by-15 inches), which may have given Carleton the impetus.

2. Francis Frith had used a 26-by-20-inch format in Egypt and Palestine, and these photographs were published in elegant, very expensive limited-edition albums. His smaller photographs and stereo views, however, reached the United States in quantity.

3. Charles B. Turrill, "An Early California Photographer: C. E. Watkins," *News Notes of California Libraries* 13 (1918): 32.

4. Oliver Wendell Holmes, "Doings of the Sunbeam," *Atlantic Monthly* 12 (1863): 8. Watkins had produced several editions of

Yosemite Valley: Photographic Views of the Falls and Valley of Yosemite in 1863, albums which measured 20½-by-26¼ inches with photographs 16-by-21 inches.

5. Hans Huth, "Yosemite, the Story of an Idea," *Sierra Club Bulletin* 33 (1948): 69–70.

6. J. D. Whitney, *Geological Survey of California*, vol. 1 (New York: Julius Bien, 1865), p. 408.

7. Watkins published twelve Mendocino views and eight photographs of the New Almaden Quicksilver Mine in an album 21-by-26½ inches, a copy of which is owned by the Huntington Library, San Marino, California. The photographs are not dated, but Turrill states that Watkins visited the mines as early as 1856 or 1857, so the views may date to that time. Carleton E. Watkins, *New Almaden Quicksilver Mine* (San Francisco, n.d.). See also J. W. Johnson, "Historical Photographs and the Coastal Engineer," *Shore and Beach* 29 (1961): 18–24.

8. William DeWitt Alexander, 5 August 1867. William DeWitt Alexander papers, Bancroft Library, University of California, Berkeley.

9. Charles R. Savage, *Philadelphia Photographer* 4 (1867): 289.

10. B. P. Avery, "Art Beginnings on the Pacific, Part II," *Overland Monthly* 1 (1868): 116.

11. He had in his employ a man of Chinese descent whom he had trained to aid him in printing. "Careful and efficient," he was also adept at " 'silvering' the old albumen paper and in the difficult chemical manipulations." Turrill, "An Early California Photographer," p. 33.

12. J. Price and C. S. Haley, comps., *The Buyers' Manual and Business Guide* (San Francisco: Francis and Valentine, 1872), p. 152.

13. It is stated in Price and Haley, *Buyers' Manual:* "For seven or eight years he [Taber] was the principal operator in one of our largest and most popular galleries." See also Ralph H. Anderson, "Carleton E. Watkins, Pioneer Photographer of the Pacific Coast," *Yosemite Nature Notes* 32 (1953): 35.

14. Watkins to Frankie [Watkins], 13 May 1880; 11 May 1880. Carleton E. Watkins papers, Yosemite National Park Research Library, Yosemite, California.

15. Carleton E. Watkins, *Arizona and Views Adjacent to the Southern Pacific Railroad* (San Francisco: c. 1880).

16. Turrill, "An Early California Photographer," p. 37.

17. The photographer produced two such folio albums for Mrs. Mollie Latham, wife of the California senator Milton Latham, and his newly cultivated patron also purchased three bound volumes of Watkins's scenic grand views with her name inscribed in gold leaf on the cover. The two albums of Thurlow Lodge, 23-by-28¼ inches, are now in the San Mateo Historical Society. The three volumes of Watkins's photographs purchased by Mrs. Latham are in the Albert Bender Rare Book Room, Stanford University, California.

18. William Henry Jackson was at this time purchasing collections for the Detroit Publishing Company and knew of Watkins's work.

19. "Views in the Yosemite Valley," *Philadelphia Photographer* 3 (1866): 106.

4. ALCATRAZ FROM NORTH BEACH, SAN FRANCISCO

5.   THE TOWN ON THE HILL. NEW ALMADEN QUICKSILVER MINE

6.   NEVADA FALL, 650 FEET. YOSEMITE   7.   YOSEMITE VALLEY : FALLS. LOWER YOSEMITE FALL

8. CASA GRANDE. PREHISTORIC RUINS

9.   BAY VIEW, SAN FRANCISCO

10.   SOUTHERN PACIFIC RAILROAD OF ARIZONA, AND CREW

11. C. P. R. R. TRANSFER BOAT "SOLANO," PORT COSTA. WAITING FOR THE TRAIN

12.   GOLDEN GATE FROM BLACK POINT, SAN FRANCISCO

13.   LASSEN'S PEAK. "CHAOS." NEVADA FLOW. 40TH PARALLEL
SURVEY. 1870

14.   OLD SOUTH SHAFT ORE QUARRY, TOUGH-NUT MINE. PART OF
TOWN OF TOMBSTONE. DRAGOON MOUNTAINS, WITH COCHISE
STRONGHOLD IN BACKGROUND, ARIZONA

15. THE ALBION

16.   TOMBSTONE M. & M. COMPANIES' DAM. 1880

17.   REAR VIEW OF TOMBSTONE M. & M. COMPANIES' 20-STAMP STEAM MILL,
LOOKING UP SAN PEDRO VALLEY, ARIZONA

18. VIEW ALONG THE VOLCANIC CHAIN, 40TH PARALLEL SURVEY. 1870

19. MOUNT SHASTA, LOOKING WESTWARD OUT THROUGH TIP OF CRATER (SHASTINA). 1870

20. SAN XAVIER MISSION, NEAR TUCSON

DR. WILLIAM A. BELL
(1841–1921)

A more unlikely applicant for the post of photographer on the Kansas Pacific Survey could not have been hired. Dr. William A. Bell,[1] graduate of Trinity College, Cambridge, and a trained physician with a practice in London, had just arrived in America, planning to visit an innovative new medical school of homeopathy in St. Louis.

He presented a letter of introduction to a geologist in Philadelphia, and then for some reason suddenly sought —and obtained—a position on the Kansas Pacific Survey. But as all other positions were filled, "a photographer alone was wanted; and as no idle man could be allowed among the party . . . I accepted the office with, I must confess, considerable diffidence, as only a fortnight remained before starting to learn an art with which I was then quite unacquainted."[2] The intrepid Dr. Bell and Timothy O'Sullivan would take to the field at almost the same time.

The Kansas Pacific Railroad sought the best southern route to the Pacific Coast. General W. W. Wright led the survey, with General William J. Palmer commanding an escort of troops for protection from the warring Plains Indians. The party assembled and waited at Fort Wallace, and the Indian uprisings became a real danger that the English doctor experienced at firsthand. He made a grisly record of a skirmish outside the fort (and perhaps had second thoughts about a western adventure).[3]

The survey got underway, however, with the doctor among the group. Once it reached the Rio Grande, the party divided into five separate contingents, each to make an accurate survey at a different latitude. Bell opted for the role of doctor-photographer with the Thirty-second Parallel group. They headed down the Purgatoire River, the doctor making side trips to Trinidad, Taos, and finally to Santa Fe in September. He stayed at the La Fonda Hotel for two weeks, converting his room into a darkroom and using the courtyard as a photographic studio: "The photographic studio was kept going all the time, and whenever I could decoy a Pueblo Indian wandering about the street, or a picturesque little black-eyed señoritta [sic], or any other study into my net, they did not escape without leaving an impression behind them. The fair sex were rather hard to manage, as they had an idea that they were turned upside down in the camera, and strongly objected to such a liberty being taken with them. Often after spending much time and trouble in collecting and forming a group, some knowing one would start this idea, and all would run for their lives, and hide."[4]

By the end of October the group arrived at that vast plateau along the designated latitude, long considered by many the most feasible route. Until then the party had enjoyed good health, and the doctor was able to move about freely. Once on the Thirty-second Parallel, how-

21.   THE RIO GRANDE DEL NORTE, NEW MEXICO. 1867

ever, the doctor wrote: "While we looked at the thick green puddle, full of creeping things, slime, and all sorts of abominations, from which we had to drink, a feeling of dread for the future involuntarily crept over us"; and he continued, "the landscape was as dreary as could well be conceived."[5] The Apaches in the region also threatened the party from time to time, about which the doctor wrote a vivid chapter for a book titled *Wonderful Adventures*.[6]

At Tucson Dr. Bell and a few traveling companions left the group and headed south to Mexico to determine if a branch railway to Guayamas might be constructed. He photographed and made notes whenever possible; everything impressed him. His description of the Mission San Xavier del Bac indicates the depth and range of his interests: "[The mission] would be considered a fine one in Switzerland or Germany. . . . How well these Indians must have worked under the Spanish missionaries to have built such a church! I have seen no other building made of furnace-baked bricks in the country; all this they must have learned. Then there was the building of the roof of brick arches, the moulding of the ornaments for the towers and decorations, and a thousand other arts necessary for the successful completion of such an undertaking."[7]

The doctor's lively narratives and descriptions continued into his Mexican adventure, where new experiences awaited him. Sleeping in a Mexican home one night, he encountered a new animal: "After much good training I thought I could have slept through anything, or in the company of any one, but I have never before tried a skunk."[8] He described tortillas, "very much like my idea of underdone chamois leather."[9] The doctor survived in good form and good humor, however, and the survey ended in Guayamas.

The spring of 1868 found Bell in the company of General Palmer, now a close friend, on a stage headed East where the doctor would depart for England. The Englishman had traveled over five thousand miles and seen remote regions of the West that few Americans had.

Dr. William A. Bell was a man of wide interests and keen intellect. Besides being an established physician at the time of his western adventure, he was a charter member of the Royal Geographical Society and the Ethnology Society in England. His official position with the survey remains as ambiguous as his original intent in joining it. Early in July, 1867, a railway official wrote to General Palmer that he "must not forget to establish the status of Mr. [Alexander] Gardner as Chief Photographer before you leave—in case your stay should be short and make him the responsible party and have *all* photographs, etc., retained for the use of the Company—Wright intimated that Dr. B. was desirous of using them for the purpose of private speculation."[10] Apparently Gardner was named official photographer, though there is no evidence he accompanied any of the advance parties. Gardner was in Kansas in the fall of 1867 making views along the newly completed rails of the Eastern Division of the Kansas Pacific, and spring of 1868 found him in Wyoming, photographing the peace conference at Fort Laramie.[11] A letter to the *Philadelphia Photographer* from Salina, Kansas, stated that "the photographer will be Dr. Bell," mentioning no other photographers with the survey.[12]

Bell was never paid by the survey for his photography, at his own request. "On leaving St. Louis I did not wish to make any agreement with the Company as to salary: had they then wanted a Physician I should have considered my degree as a sufficient guaranty, but as a photographer I was of doubtful value and suffered being considered so."[13] Still, the doctor came away with what he wanted—a western adventure complete with photographic evidence.[14]

Bell returned to England and immediately set to work producing two volumes about the American West, which appeared in 1869. In his foreword to *New Tracks in North America*, the doctor-turned-writer expressed the hope that the books would be of interest to "the man of science, the lover of adventure and the practical public," both English and American.

While many books of travel and adventure written by foreign visitors to America existed, Dr. Bell's volumes became widely read. They dealt with an incredible range of subject matter, enough to satisfy any interest—ethnology, botany, physical geography, wildlife—and he wove a thoroughly engrossing tale of adventure and human interest as well. He described the wide range of characters he encountered and made observations on everything from the liberated state of women in Kansas ("the Paradise of Petticoats") to the rhythm of the railway workers as they laid the tracks. The unique illustrations for the volumes, both lithographs and woodcuts, were derived from his photographs. These, in themselves rather primitive, were thrilling in reproduction. The books quickly went into a second printing and the work was translated into German.

It is not known what use the company made of the original photographs, if any. A railway official complained: "The pictures taken by Dr. Bell are not of much account. Most of them are too dim or not well finished and the photographer here complains much of the negative and says the result is caused by carelessness" (and perhaps two weeks training).[15]

Apparently, once the doctor published his books, he abandoned both his profession of medicine and his avocation, photography. He moved to the American West to become vice-president of the Denver and Rio Grande Railroad, settling in Colorado Springs, where he built a large estate named Briarhurst.[16] The transplanted Englishman became a powerful force in the development of the region, and "like the miner, the land-hungry squatter, and the riverfront drifter, the transient once again influenced the course of western development."[17] He wrote several articles to interest transatlantic investors and settlers in the West, assuring them that "the latest Eastern improvements are at once adopted in the West where you find a far higher average of intelligence and in the case of Colorado and California, of social refinement than is to be met with anywhere except in the long-established cities of the Atlantic sea-board."[18]

Yet the doctor never quite became a westerner, and in 1890 he resigned his position with the railway to return to Kent, England. The peripatetic Bell came back to America on business several times and settled again at Briarhurst during World War I, but he returned to England at the war's conclusion and remained there until his death at the age of eighty.

Dr. William A. Bell's books reached a wide audience,

as did his articles, and today they are considered by historians to be not only some of the most useful but among the most engaging and well-written early accounts of the West. The sum of his brief photographic career arrived in a package at the State Historical Society of Colorado in the form of a few dozen oval photographs, but the full impact of that amateur photographic venture can only be guessed.

NOTES

1. Dr. William A. Bell has often been confused with the photographer William Bell, who accompanied the Wheeler survey for the 1872 season. Terry Mangan, formerly of the State Historical Society of Colorado, Denver, was the first to make the distinction clear.

2. William A. Bell, *New Tracks in North America*, 2 vols. (London: Chapman & Hall, 1869–70), 1: xvi.

3. Bell described the scene: "I have seen in days gone by sights horrible and gory—death in all its forms of agony and distortion—but never did I feel the sickening sensation, the giddy, fainting feeling that came over me when I saw our dead, dying and wounded after this Indian fight. A handful of men, to be sure, but with enough wounds upon them to have slain a company, if evenly distributed. . . . Sergeant Wylyams [*sic*] lay dead beside his horse; and as the fearful picture first met my gaze, I was horror-stricken. Horse and rider were stripped bare of trapping and clothes, while around them the trampled, blood-stained ground showed the desperation of the struggle." Bell, *New Tracks*, 1: 61–62.

4. Ibid., 1: 148.

5. Ibid., 2: 36–37.

6. William A. Bell, "Ten Days' Journey in Southern Arizona," in *Wonderful Adventures, A Series of Narratives of Personal Experiences Among the Native Tribes of America* (Philadelphia: William B. Evans & Co., 1874).

7. Bell, *New Tracks*, 2: 98–99.

8. Ibid., p. 109.

9. Ibid., p. 118.

10. Charles B. Lamborn to Gen. W. J. Palmer, 31 July 1867. William A. Bell papers, State Historical Society of Colorado.

11. Alexander Gardner published a large portfolio of original photographs from this excursion titled *Across the Continent on the Kansas Pacific Railroad* (Washington, D.C.: n.d.).

12. *Philadelphia Photographer* 4 (1867): 266.

13. Bell to Gen. W. J. Palmer, 23 October 1867. Bell papers, State Historical Society of Colorado.

14. The doctor apparently sent twenty-seven negatives to Gardner and later wrote to him requesting copies; Gardner told him he "forgot to take them with him to Washington." When Bell wrote to him in Washington, he received no reply. Bell eventually received the prints through Palmer whom he wrote, "I never want [them] into Gardiners [*sic*] hands." Bell to Palmer, 23 October 1867. Bell papers, State Historical Society of Colorado.

15. Lamborn to Palmer, 31 July 1867. Bell papers, State Historical Society of Colorado.

16. Mrs. Bell later furnished Briarhurst with, among other things, Thomas Moran's *Mountain of the Holy Cross*, which she purchased in England.

17. Robert V. Hine, *The American West: An Interpretive History* (Boston: Little, Brown and Co., 1973), p. 264.

18. W. J. Palmer and W. A. Bell, *The Development and Colonization of the "Great West"* (London: Chapman & Hall, 1874).

22.   HOT SPRINGS AT OJO CALIENTE. 1867

23. CITY OF ROCKS, RIO MIEMBRES. 1867

24.   CAMP SCENE ALONG THE 32ND PARALLEL, KANSAS-PACIFIC SURVEY. 1867

TIMOTHY H. O'SULLIVAN
(1840 – 1882)

He understood the bone-weary stance that generals and men alike confided to the camera; he knew the look of suffering, fear, and desperation; he had photographed the bloom of life, cut down as once wheat stalks had been, at Gettysburg.

Timothy O'Sullivan had not simply observed the war, he had campaigned.[1] He had traveled with the Army of the Potomac to almost every major battle and finally to Appomattox, photographing the war to its conclusion. It was said the lean Irishman tempted death on too many occasions, but he survived the Civil War. His performance left little doubt as to his ability and character. When stillness finally came at Appomattox in 1865, the twenty-five-year-old photographer returned to Washington, D.C., with Alexander Gardner. They began to prepare a photographic album of the Civil War, each volume consisting of one hundred mounted prints, nearly half of them from O'Sullivan's negatives.[2]

O'Sullivan had yet to meet the brilliant geologist, two years his junior, who was suggesting to Congress one of the most ingenious and far-ranging surveys of the West. Clarence King proposed to make a scientific reconnaissance of the geological structure, geographical condition, and natural resources along the Fortieth Parallel from California to the plains. To accomplish his aims he was allowed virtually to dictate his own orders and hire a staff entirely of his choosing. He selected specialists rather than all-purpose generalists, a group of highly educated young men many of whom would later be reckoned among America's great scientists. Among his first appointments was a specialist in field photography, Timothy O'Sullivan.

By training and education the two made unlikely companions. O'Sullivan's immigrant origins were in marked contrast to the wellborn King;[3] the photographer's only education derived from the Brady galleries, while the cosmopolitan geologist had been among the first graduates of the Sheffield School of Science at Yale. O'Sullivan's expertise had been formed from experience and shaped under fire while the dilettante King was deciding his future career by reading books ranging from scientific treatises to Ruskin.[4] In character, however, the pair shared a deep kinship, for the intellectual geologist had a reckless side to his nature that "placed less value on his reputation as a scientist than on his credit as 'a fellow not easily scared.' "[5] In that, O'Sullivan was his match.

At first King's group of educated "youngsters" found O'Sullivan somewhat a bore, for he did not share their intellectual or philosophical pursuits. William Bailey complained: "His chief fault is his reminiscences of the Potomac Army. . . . One would think he had slept with Grant and Meade and was the direct confident of Stanton."[6] The scientists gained appreciation for his person-

25. KING SURVEY. 1867. SAND DUNE NEAR SAND SPRINGS, NEVADA

al qualities and abilities as the survey progressed, however, for he was precisely the kind of man needed to make useful pictures for their purposes. He consistently carried out his assignments, no matter the difficulty; he worked well with the geologists and followed their orders; he was competent, though technically his negatives are not of comparable quality to other survey photographers. More important, O'Sullivan could be counted on, whatever the personal risk.

The goal set for the first survey season was the examination of fifteen thousand square miles across Nevada. The party of about seventeen set out in the summer of 1867 for a land absolutely wild and unexplored. The photographer, with the aid of an experienced packer, outfitted a mule-powered Civil War-type ambulance. Thus equipped with the tools of his profession, he fell into the procession as they headed east from Sacramento.

Once in Nevada a vast, forbidding landscape stretched before them that did little to dispel the myth of the "Great American Desert." The survey party set to work, establishing a base camp from which smaller groups could spread to collect data. O'Sullivan documented these jumping-off points—the self-conscious, often sheepish expressions on the faces of the members giving the impression that the group was obviously gathered for the record rather than caught in the act—and trekked over western Nevada with various side parties. He went from the Humboldt Range to the Sink, down the Truckee River, and on to the alkaline Pyramid Lake, his mule laden with glass plates and chemicals to be synthesized into images.

Obstacles constantly impeded the photographic effort. The barren land provided a ceaseless shower of dust and fine sand, but very little water in which to develop negatives. Then, on the Truckee River, which had never been navigated, they nearly drowned in the stuff. In a courageous act which could have cost him his life, O'Sullivan swam ashore to secure the boat, which had jammed against the rocks and crushed the oars.

Worse physical afflictions waited in the Humboldt Sink. Blazing heat and waves of mosquitoes engulfed the party, leaving them swollen and ill with the "mountain ail."[7] At one point only O'Sullivan and one of the topographers, along with three camp men, were strong enough to do a day's duty; but O'Sullivan hassled his 9 1/2-by-11-inch camera, dealt with his cranky mules (and sometimes equally cranky packer), and worked his chemicals as best he could.

The party welcomed winter, one group quartered in Virginia City, the other in Carson City. In late summer O'Sullivan had photographed the assortment of shacks and saloons among the hills that called itself Virginia City. In January, King called him to photograph the subterranean aspect of the town—the Comstock Lode. Apparently magnesium had never been tried in the gaseous underworld of a mine, but the daring Irishman ignited the highly flammable substance hundreds of feet in the earth and made what are believed to be the first photographs of a mine interior.[8] The venture produced an evocative set of images.

Winter, and King's ebullient presence, restored health and enthusiasm for the next season's work. With a new member, the painter John Henry Hill, the explorations proceeded across an area that embraced rank upon rank of parallel mountain ranges. O'Sullivan's group began a midsummer crossing of the high divides which proved to be unbelievably strenuous. Snowdrifts of up to thirty feet would swallow the party in an instant. The men and animals were frequently lost from sight, and then would begin the digging out. In one instance it took thirteen hours to cross a divide of about two and one-half miles. They traveled at night, hoping that the icy, rarefied air had frozen the snow sufficiently hard to bear the weight of their crossing.

Mid-September found the photographer with King, heading toward the basin of the Snake River to study reported coal finds. Miles before the black canyons and falls born of the serpentine wanderings of the Snake appeared, their presence was felt. "You ride upon a waste," wrote King, "the pale earth stretched in desolation. Suddenly you stand upon a brink. As if the earth had yawned, black walls flank the abyss. Deep in the bed a great river fights its way through the labyrinth of blackened ruins, and plunges in foaming whiteness over a cliff of lava. You turn from the brink as from a frightful glimpse of the Inferno, and when you have gone a mile the earth seems to have closed again. Every trace of the canon [sic] has vanished, and the stillness of the desert reigns."[9] Once there, the falls arranged themselves into endless images in O'Sullivan's ground glass; he photographed them repeatedly, exuberantly, over the ten days the party camped on the canyon's brink. One senses his excitement: "There is in the entire region of the falls such wildness of beauty that a feeling pervades the mind almost unconsciously that you are, if not the *first* white man who has ever trod that trail, certainly one of the very few who have ventured so far."[10] For O'Sullivan, it made a triumphant end to another difficult season.

Appropriations—and men—were exhausted at the end of the two-year survey, but the group required more time. King headed for Washington carrying many of O'Sullivan's images with him and returned with more money for what he thought to be a final season in the field.

Clarence King led the first foray of the 1869 survey into the dreary alkaline areas surrounding the great Salt Lake. The group ventured northward, into the barren reaches of the snow-covered Wasatch and Uinta Mountains. They surveyed throughout the summer, O'Sullivan photographing the valleys, mountains, lakes, and canyons. At the Green River divide, set as the eastern limit, King declared the three-year survey finished. The members returned East and set about preparing and analyzing their findings in carefully thought-out reports; in the meantime, they showed O'Sullivan's photographs, images which excited great interest. The impact of the visual record was felt by the other survey leaders, and in fact each would make more extensive use of their photographic images than King ever did.

King's use of the photographs indicates that he did not consider them an end in themselves. He placed sets of the photographs in the hands of the scientists as visual records—factual, documentary evidence to refer to as they prepared their findings—but he never bothered to produce a uniform set of captions for the portfolios. The photographs were mounted on 18-by-24-inch mats that bore the survey title, but King neither bound them into a handsome volume, as Ferdinand Hayden did with the Yellowstone views, nor did he publish the photographs in a separate edition as Lieutenant George M. Wheeler would.[11] Nor did King use the photographs to illustrate his final reports. He had lithographs made from them instead, explaining to General A. A. Humphreys: "It is my intention to give to this work a finish which will place it on an equal footing with the best European publications."[12]

By the time King was ordered to return to the field in 1870, O'Sullivan had accepted a position with Commander T. O. Selfridge in quest of a canal route in the jungles near the Isthmus of Darien (Panama).[13] Once there, steaming humidity and torrential rains rendered plates and chemicals unstable and the density of the jungle made viewpoints impossible. O'Sullivan relinquished the position of survey photographer to John Moran, and the summer of 1871 found the photographer back in the West in the employ of Lieutenant George M. Wheeler, who planned to survey an area that embraced 993,360 square miles of mountainous terrain and 450,000 square miles of plains. In Wheeler rested the army's hopes to survive and rival the serious competition that civilian scientists posed. The army, reduced to incredibly small numbers, also needed accurate maps of the Southwest, not only to ascertain "the selection of such sites as may be of use for future military operations or occupation," but also to know where the Indians were, their numbers, and anything else that might help them to pursue and subdue the Indian population. Much of the proposed survey area was considered "the Botany Bay of military banishment," but Wheeler, anxious to make a name for himself in the tradition of the pre-Civil War soldier-engineer explorers, welcomed the assignment.[14]

Wheeler equaled King both in age and ambition, but his approach was military. While many of the civilian group found the young West Pointer intolerable, one surmises that Timothy O'Sullivan had no difficulty in adapting to Wheeler's leadership. He produced some of his best images during the three years that he stayed with the lieutenant. Wheeler, as did King, held the photographer in high regard, often placing him in charge of a smaller field party and referring to him as "executive in charge."

Wheeler also assembled an impressive group of scientists and—to publicize the explorations as they took place—a writer, Frederick Loring, of whom O'Sullivan made a striking portrait. He would last one season and meet with a tragic fate, taking with him many of his photographer-friend's negatives.

Gathered at Halleck Station in May, the thirty men headed south through Nevada, crossing, recrossing, and circling their way to the southern tip. O'Sullivan drove his photographic ambulance over mile after mile of scorched, arid earth and volcanic rubble. In July the party arrived in Death Valley. A searing landscape stretched before them in almost overwhelming 120-degree heat.

At Camp Mohave, Lieutenant Wheeler announced

that they would commence explorations of the Colorado River by traveling upstream. It sounded like an idea conjured up by army officials manning desks rather than oars, but Wheeler believed the survey objectives could not be accomplished by a rapid reconnaissance down the river. O'Sullivan recorded the September departure, then moved out in a boat christened the "Picture."

Much of the Colorado River had been explored by previous and concurrent expeditions, but all that was visually known of the Grand Canyon at that time devolved from the fantastic visions drawn by F. W. von Egloffstein. O'Sullivan became the first photographer to intercept on his glass some of the exotic, awesome scenes.

Slowly the party gained against the current, O'Sullivan photographing from point to point as they moved upstream. They reached Black Canyon, where Timothy made evocative images of the river threading its way through dark, vertical canyon walls. Their upward journey became more difficult; the water coursed rougher and whiter the further they traveled. As they began their ascent into the Grand Canyon they hit rapids, which Wheeler with military understatement described as "more formidable than any yet seen." Only O'Sullivan's swimming ability and courage saved a boat caught in the rapids. Yet, after exhausting days of trekking upstream, the photographer set about making views. His photograph entitled "Grand Canyon" was taken from a considerable height on the opposite bank of the river from camp.

At a point aptly named Disaster Rapids a boat capsized, consigning Wheeler's notes and collections to the river bottom, not to mention some of the few rations left. Wheeler, threatened with the prospect of starvation, mutiny, and perhaps worse rapids ahead, sent two men to locate a relief party and led one final, exhausting push to reach the rendezvous point. The group that straggled ashore numbered about half the original contingent, O'Sullivan among them. Realizing the perils to Wheeler's party, it seems miraculous that O'Sullivan's nearly three hundred glass plates survived. To learn that the principal ones in the collection perished a few weeks later on the Butterfield stagecoach with Loring, as they headed for Washington, is an unbelievable irony. The few negatives that survived are those O'Sullivan kept with him, for whatever fateful reason.

O'Sullivan left the 1872 Wheeler survey to Philadelphia photographer William Bell, and rejoined Clarence King, who was making a last reconnaissance along the entire length of the Fortieth Parallel. The photographer joined the payroll at 150 dollars a month in April and worked through November, making both stereo and full-plate views. He would then have been unemployed but for the fact that Bell left Wheeler's survey after only one season.

O'Sullivan returned to the Wheeler survey in 1873 at the salary of 175 dollars a month. The photographic effort remained a major expense,[15] but Wheeler made extensive use of the images. The photographer covered a vast area in the next years, documenting the mountains, deserts, and their inhabitants. He was among the first to photograph the marvelous structures in the Canyon de Chelly. His images of White House Ruin, posed like a stage set, became the first of countless views that would follow.

As far as is known, when Timothy O'Sullivan finished the field explorations with the Wheeler survey in 1875 he left the West forever. In 1879 Clarence King took over the directorship of the United States Geological Survey, and he immediately hired his old comrade of survey days as the first photographer, but King was severely restricted in his goals that first year by small appropriations. The following year, O'Sullivan applied for a photographic position with the Treasury Department in Washington, D.C. Impressive recommendations poured in on his behalf—from Mathew Brady; from Wheeler, who wrote that he was a "fine photographer, a man of unquestionable integrity and executive ability"; from Major John Wesley Powell, attesting to his "great skill with a camera"; and from Clarence King, who sent a three-page letter of praise. Few could have matched such references. Timothy began work immediately, but by March, 1881, he had to resign because of a worsening tubercular condition. He died of the disease the following year, leaving no heirs to receive or remember the images he had made at enormous personal sacrifice.

O'Sullivan's style had changed significantly from his Civil War work, due in large measure to the new land in which he found himself: it matched and challenged his sense of toughness and masculinity, and these elements are unmistakable in his work. His photographs more than met the contract, going beyond the needs of the survey to record the topography of the land, both its natural and man-made features, and the event of the expedition itself. What O'Sullivan himself intended in his pictures beyond an accurate record for scientific purposes, what they meant to him beyond the sheer accomplishment of making them under extreme conditions, is impossible to conjecture.

Unlike other photographers of the early West, O'Sullivan responded with an innate feeling for contour and the abstract forms of terrain and rock. Whether photographing the sharp defiles of the Virginia mountains, the vertical canyon walls of the Colorado River, or the geological formations of Utah, the contour is the subject. His strongest point of focus inevitably falls upon the brightest line of adjacency, where light and dark meet and one perceives maximum contrast, a perception heightened by the inverted ground-glass image.

His compositions are by no means simple. He composed his pictorial elements well, often in complex asymmetrical patterns. He used the foreground with skill, in some cases weighting it to give a sense of depth to the scene, in others placing objects near the front to render scale, but his images are neither stylized nor self-conscious. Massing becomes a variation of shades, from semidark to sun-bright reflections, revealing texture and pattern, and the flat, bleached effect of the sky makes the rock shapes bolder and more dominant, the statement even more stark. In the painters' West, the rich, deep skies create a mood and aura of beauty; in O'Sullivan's photographs, the blank sky, devoid of clouds and elements, imparts the feeling of a blazing sun, parching and searing the landscape. It was the way he experienced much of the land he was called upon to photograph.

O'Sullivan moved less easily among the man-made topographical intrusions on the landscape. When he photographed the mining town of Virginia City, his views appear violated by the ticky-tack geometries of crude shacks, forms unrelated to the land. Unlike either Carleton Watkins, who skillfully composed the man-made into his middle ground and utilized the forms to optimum benefit, or Jack Hillers, whose pueblos rhythmically and compositionally relate to the landscape, O'Sullivan's mining town views are rather more like collages, with the forms pasted on.

A bit of a braggart among the men, O'Sullivan reveals a self-consciousness when he stands behind the camera—there is an uneasiness on both sides. His camp pictures are well enough done, but stiff and undistinguished. When he photographs the Indians with his stereo camera, they appear as wooden as their expressions, their poses and demeanor absolutely frozen. But when he is in his element—the vastness of the West—his picture-making is strong, consistent, vital.

Timothy O'Sullivan's visions of the West were not appealing images in their time, for they evoke an aesthetic scarcely visible in the art of the period. It is doubtful that Clarence King, later a connoisseur of art and collector of Turner paintings, thought of O'Sullivan's photographs in artistic terms. Though he was by far the most sophisticated and cultured of the survey leaders, it was not he who submitted O'Sullivan's work to the International Exposition in Vienna in 1873, but Wheeler. (The English and Europeans passed over O'Sullivan's work without mention. Eadweard Muybridge swept the honors that year with his Yosemite photographs.)

What seemed in their period a record of rocks, taken with geological purpose, has become for us an almost metaphysical series of images. Timothy O'Sullivan's work strikes a contemporary chord, touching sophisticated twentieth-century artistic sensibilities. His strange sense of the wilderness sometimes borders on the surreal, and the abstraction of forms has an ambiguity, like an unfinished painting with only the bold outlines sketched in, the forms shaded with a poster-like flatness. His rare, lonely perceptions of sand dunes remind us of the moonscapes only recently seen. They evoke a similar lunar silence—of a place without time or atmosphere, forbidding and uninhabitable, with no sign of life.

NOTES

1. In his application to the Treasury Department, O'Sullivan stated that he had served six months as a first lieutenant and then three years as a "civilian photographer" with the Army of the Potomac. For detailed information on his Civil War career, see James D. Horan, *Timothy O'Sullivan: America's Forgotten Photographer* (Garden City, N.Y.: Doubleday & Co., Inc., 1966).

2. Alexander Gardner, *Gardner's Photographic Sketch Book of the War* (Washington, D.C.: Philip & Solomons, 1865–66).

3. O'Sullivan's death certificate states his birthplace as Ireland, although a letter regarding the Treasury Department position states, "I am a native of the state of New York." Reproduced in Horan, *Timothy O'Sullivan.*

4. Henry Adams referred to Clarence King as "the most many-

sided genius of his day." Thurman Wilkins, *Clarence King* (New York: Macmillan Co., 1958), p. 6.

5. Ibid., p. 4.

6. William Bailey to Lode [Loring Woart Bailey], 14 August 1867. Bailey papers, Huntington Library, San Marino, California.

7. John Samson, "Photographs from the High Rockies," *Harper's New Monthly Magazine* 39 (1869): 471.

8. In the previous year, the Mammoth Caves had been photographed successfully and articles on the use of magnesium wire had appeared regularly in the *Philadelphia Photographer* since December, 1865, when the first portraits by magnesium light had been made. See *Philadelphia Photographer* 2 (1865): 189–90.

9. Clarence King, "The Falls of the Shoshone," *Overland Monthly* 5 (1870): 385.

10. Samson, "Photographs from the High Rockies," p. 475.

11. King did use O'Sullivan's photographs to illustrate his poetry in a special Christmas book he had printed for his sister and her playmates. Clarence King, *The Three Lakes: Marian, Lall, and Jan, and How They Were Named*, 1870.

12. King to Gen. A. A. Humphreys, 25 February 1874. Fortieth Parallel Survey Records, Record Group 57, National Archives, Washington, D.C.

13. Carleton E. Watkins, it may be recalled, served with King on the 1870 survey.

14. George M. Wheeler, *Report Upon United States Geographical Surveys West of the One Hundredth Meridian* (Washington, D.C.: Government Printing Office, 1889), vol. I: 163.

15. Wheeler's voucher for the second quarter of 1873 alone lists $1,152.50 paid to the Scovill Manufacturing Company for photographic equipment. Expenditure vouchers, Surveys West of the 100th Meridian, Record Group 77, National Archives, Washington, D.C.

26.　WHEELER EXPEDITION. 1871. BLACK CANYON, COLORADO RIVER, LOOKING
BELOW FROM CAMP 7

27.　GREEN RIVER CANYONS. VERMILLION CREEK CANYON, LOOKING DOWN-
STREAM OUT TO BROWN'S PARK. KING SURVEY

28. WHEELER EXPEDITION. 1873. CHURCH OF SAN MIGUEL, SANTA FE, NEW MEXICO

29. WHEELER EXPEDITION. 1871. WALL IN THE GRAND CANYON, COLORADO RIVER

30. WHEELER EXPEDITION. LOGAN SPRINGS, NEVADA

31. WHEELER EXPEDITION. 1873. ANCIENT DWELLING IN
CANYON DE CHELLY (WHITE HOUSE RUIN)

32. WHEELER EXPEDITION. 1871. BLACK CANYON, COLORADO RIVER, LOOKING
ABOVE FROM CAMP 8

33. UPPER COLORADO CAMP, WALLS 600 FEET HIGH. 1871

34. KING SURVEY. 1868. CAMP SCENE, RUBY VALLEY, NEVADA

35. KING SURVEY. 1868. IN THE GOULD AND CURRY MINE,
COMSTOCK LODE, NEVADA

EADWEARD MUYBRIDGE
(1830–1904)

As Leland Stanford struck the last spike at Promontory Point in 1869, he triggered an instantaneous electromagnetic signal to the telegraph that confirmed, without words, the joining of the rails.[1] A few years later, the same principle would be applied to the camera shutter by Eadweard Muybridge, working in collaboration with Stanford, to document beyond doubt the "Attitudes of Animals in Motion."[2] The photographer later wrote with characteristic éclat, "The circumstances must have been exceptionally felicitous that made co-laborateurs of the man that no practical impediment could halt and of the artist who, to keep pace with the demands of the railroad builder, hurried his art to a marvel of perfection that it is fair to believe it would not else have reached in another century."[3]

Solid middle-class English by birth and inventive by nature, the well-educated Muybridge came to America in 1851 as the employee of an English publishing firm. He traveled widely, and among his acquaintances was the daguerreotypist Silas Selleck, who may have initiated him into the art.[4]

Like countless others, Selleck among them, Muybridge succumbed to the lure of California. He established a bookstore in the new metropolis of San Francisco. His business acumen combined with his energy quickly shaped a going concern, but he remained an agent for a London publishing house as well. He became a substantial member of the community, joining the Mercantile Library Association, and as his business flourished he sent for younger brothers to man the store while he traveled about the state in search of both literary and visual material.

When he decided to return to his homeland in 1860, Muybridge chose to make part of the journey by stagecoach. He survived more than two thousand miles of hard-springed coach travel, as well as heat, fatigue, and thirst, but as the Butterfield stage raced through Texas the coach went out of control and overturned. Muybridge was thrown clear but seriously injured. Home in England, he engaged the eminent physician Sir William Gull, who espoused natural therapy. Full recovery took several years, the same years during which the United States was absorbed in civil struggle. Eventually the energy Muybridge seemed ever able to summon returned, and he later wrote he had "been diligently, and at the same time studiously engaged in photography."[5]

By 1867 Muybridge prepared to venture forth to the New World once again. From all reports he had changed, not only in profession but in personality and appearance. He seemed eccentric and irascible. His friend Silas Selleck stated that before Muybridge left for Europe, Eadweard had been a "genial, pleasant and quick business-

36.   ANCIENT GLACIER CHANNEL. 1872

man; after his return from Europe he was very eccentric and so unlike his way before going." Another friend commented: "He was much more irritable after his return, much more careless in his dress and was not such a good businessman. . . . He has not been the same man in any respect since."[6]

Immediately upon his return, Muybridge went into competition with the best photographers of the city. With a flair for the dramatic he styled himself "Helios" and drove his "Flying Studio" (a one-horse wagon sporting an emblematic camera with wings) to Yosemite. On his first outing, Helios made 6-by-8-inch and stereo photographs and advertised: "For artistic effect, and careful manipulation, they are pronounced by all the best landscape painters and photographers in the city to be the most exquisite photographic views ever produced on this coast."[7] Doubtful, considering that Watkins had won a first prize for his large Yosemite landscapes—but Muybridge, ever his own best publicist, was undaunted. Some of his work did have a striking difference, however: clouds and atmospheric effects. To accomplish this Muybridge claimed to have devised a lateral "sky-shade" which gradated exposure times for the sky, middle ground, and foreground. Thus atmospheric effects could be printed in from a second negative more successfully. Considering the lateral design of his shade, it would have been effective only in simple compositions with a rather straight, definite horizon line, for if irregular contours intruded into the sky, correct exposure of both elements would have been impossible. But the device undoubtedly reduced the flare factor of an overexposed sky on the total negative, and the design illustrates the photographer's early concern with innovative technical photographic devices.

In the same brochure, Muybridge mentions almost as an afterthought an invention of more practical importance—a specially designed cloth that covered the back of the camera. The cloth, with a black side to the camera and a white side to reflect sunlight, kept the plateholder light-tight and cooler. Light leakage, one of the major problems in using large-format cameras, was thus held to a minimum, and Muybridge devised an attached sleeve through which one could pull the holder to expose the wet plate.

During the next five years he plunged into a flurry of activity, taking at least two thousand photographs. He made nature studies—trees, clouds, and atmospheric effects—and made photographs for several United States government departments. He even traveled to Alaska, among the first photographers to do so.

In 1872 Muybridge received a telegram from the horsebreeder-trainer Leland Stanford, who was also president of the Central Pacific Railroad and governor of California. Stanford wanted Muybridge to attempt to photograph a horse in motion, a very bold and original idea.

Muybridge went to Stanford's home to attempt the photographic record. He had a lens with a maximum aperture approximately f8; wet-plate collodion with extremely slow emulsion speeds; and no workable shutter mechanism. He later claimed that he had captured Occident, Stanford's prize horse, "while trotting, laterally in front of his camera at rates of speed varying from two minutes and twenty-five seconds to two minutes and eighteen seconds per mile." He further claimed that the results of his few days' efforts in 1872 "were sufficiently sharp to give a recognizable silhouette. . . . So far as the immediate point at issue was concerned, the object of the experiment was accomplished."[8] Given the reciprocity failure of collodion-based film and its exposure time, he would have been fortunate to obtain even a blur on his plate, but the experiment whetted his appetite to try again. In April, 1873, he returned to repeat the effort.

He claimed to have contrived a shutter, triggered with a tensioned spring, that opened and closed within 1/500 second. This calculation is virtually impossible, since the shutter was mechanically triggered (known data on today's most sophisticated mechanical shutters indicate that the upper limit of dependability is 1/1000 second). The newspaper *Alta California* further reported in its issue of April 7 that the photographer had succeeded in obtaining "a perfect likeness of the celebrated horse . . . the spokes of the sulky were caught as if they were not in motion." Again, neither the materials nor equipment available to him warrant credibility. For his part, Muybridge claimed that the photographs "give a recognizable silhouette portrait of the driver and some of them exhibited the horse with all four of his feet clearly lifted, at the same time, above the surface of the ground."[9] The horse was trotting on white sheets, so it is possible that the contrasts registered on the negative, but if Muybridge obtained anything more than a shadow it would be remarkable.

In the meantime Muybridge continued with his Yosemite series, in obvious competition to Watkins, offering forty views for one hundred dollars. By 1872 new trails had been built throughout the Yosemite and the energetic Muybridge determined to cover every area—upper rim and surrounding high country to the valley floor—with a 20-by-24-inch camera.

Muybridge obtained some views by sheer daring, like having himself lowered by rope down onto precipices; he obtained other images by cutting down trees that interfered with his view. His large photographs (17-by-24 inches) of Yosemite netted him not only a handsome income but also acclaim as the leading photographer in San Francisco. On this trip, he also made smaller format pictures, in subject series of rivers, atmospheric effects, and trees, and these also proved highly salable. His five busy years of photography had earned him a reputation for which he had worked very hard. He was awarded an International Gold Medal for landscape in Vienna.

Though in fact many of the views taken by Muybridge and Watkins are easily mistaken, Muybridge offered a number of new vantage points. Muybridge also turned his photographic talents to reportage. He packed his gear and headed for the lava beds near the California-Oregon border where the Modoc warriors were making their final stand against the army (which outnumbered them nearly seven to one). Muybridge's photographs of the event are static—war as yet could not be waged and won before a wet plate—the scenes strained and contrived.

Amidst his busy career Muybridge, forty-two, married a woman half his age. He was drawn to attractive people, and petite, blond Flora, who traveled in theatrical circles, held a certain intrigue for the aesthete and piqued his flair for the dramatic. Beyond that, they shared few interests or intellectual pursuits. Soon Flora fell in love with a dashing young soldier of fortune, Harry Larkyns, who possessed all the charm and *joie de vivre* that her older, ambition-driven husband did not. It was only a matter of time and gossip before Muybridge realized they were lovers. Larkyns left San Francisco, but the situation was further complicated when Flora bore a child and evidence seemed to indicate that Larkyns might be its father. Muybridge found Larkyns and shot him to death.

His trial unfolded like a play, sensational and dramatic. There was no question that Muybridge had committed murder, so the defense argued that a man wronged had the right to vengeance. The all-male jury agreed, and Muybridge was acquitted. But the trial took its toll on him personally, and he decided to absent himself from San Francisco. He negotiated with the Pacific Mail Steamship Company to make photographs in Panama and Central America, and, less than two weeks after the verdict, he was on his way.

With the transcontinental railroad completed in 1869, the East-West route via the Isthmus of Panama was largely abandoned. Muybridge set out to re-create the area as a tourist's delight, to photograph "all the curious places that a traveller by Railroad and Pacific Mail Company's ship can see or be within reach of," as a Panamanian paper reported.

Central America yielded fine views to the brooding Muybridge. He photographed landscapes possessing a strangeness and a moody, mysterious beauty, and architectural subjects as well. At the same time, the redoubtable camera man experimented with a shutter for instantaneous photographs.

Scandal assuaged, Muybridge returned to San Francisco late in 1875, and in 1876 Leland Stanford again commissioned him to experiment with photography of motion. Once more the attempts produced doubtful results in terms of a recognizable image, but, repeating the experiment in 1877, Muybridge announced that an "automatic electro-photograph" of Occident trotting had been produced. This time he claimed an exposure of 1/1000 second, but a fast shutter, even if he possessed it, would not have worked on collodion.

Muybridge sent a photograph of Occident trotting to the editor of *Alta California* (2 August) and unabashedly stated: "The picture has been retouched, as is customary at this time with all first-class photographic work, for the purpose of giving a better effect to the details. In every other respect, the photograph is exactly as it was made in the camera." In fact, the photograph was a copy of an artist's painting; the only actual photographic image was the face of the driver, which had been pasted to the canvas. This fact was discovered when a large exhibition of Muybridge photographs was being prepared by the Stanford University Museum of Art staff in 1972. The painting is owned by that museum. While the painting may have been based on photographic evidence, the claim was fraudulent.

But the photographer vindicated himself the following year (1878) when experimentation began in earnest. Stanford sought hard data on animal locomotion to provide a scientific basis for animal training. Toward that end, he committed everything necessary—men, material, labor— and a huge sum of money.

The investigation moved to the Palo Alto Stock Farm, where equipment began to be assembled. A dozen stereoscopic cameras were ordered from Scovill in New York, the double lenses to fit them from John Henry Dallmeyer in London. (Because of the small format of the stereo camera, it was possible to use lenses of a shorter focal length which had greater light-gathering power. This reduced the exposure time.) Muybridge prepared a rough experimental model for the proposed study, derived in part from a theoretical scheme postulated by the British photographer O. G. Rejlander,[10] and Stanford made available Central Pacific Railroad technicians, engineers, and shops for the actual construction of needed apparatus. Muybridge apparently made a rough sketch for a shutter to which John D. Isaacs contributed the idea of using an electromagnetic triggering mechanism.

Inexplicably, Muybridge continued to use the wet-plate collodion process rather than dry plates, though several English firms were producing the latter commercially at that time. While controversy raged over dry versus wet plates, the success of Muybridge's effort rested on obtaining the fastest exposure possible rather than on pictorial print quality; the dry plate would surely have made a significant difference.

With the aid of specialists translating Muybridge's model into form, the stage was set along the one-mile track in Palo Alto in June, 1878. Twelve cameras, twenty-one inches apart, faced a wooden backdrop demarcated into consecutively numbered segments. Threads con-nected to the shutter-release mechanism (a catch held the shutter blade in place in front of the lens until released by the electromagnet) stretched across the track so that as the traveling horse broke the thread, the slit of the shutter dropped across the lens.

The press was assembled. Sleek Abe Edgington galloped along the track at forty feet per second and tripped the mechanisms of the twelve cameras. Muybridge and assistants immediately developed the twelve plates, taken in less than half a second, before the wondering eyes of the spectators, who saw the negatives only a few minutes after the event. The response ranged from disbelief to acclaim, and the event engendered worldwide interest and reverberations. This time the photographs existed; there was tangible, available proof.

Muybridge quickly applied for patents on his "Method and Apparatus for Photographing Objects in Motion," and continued photographing Stanford's horses for the remainder of 1878. He copyrighted and published a series of six cards, "The Horse in Motion," which pictured six, eight, or twelve positions. Earlier suspicions abated. Thomas Eakins, among others, bought a set, and though the prints were rather more like silhouettes, they did clearly disclose various postures, arresting movement at each minute stage of a trot, gallop, or walk. Published in *Scientific American* in October, 1878, and in the European publication *La Nature* in December of the same year, they were hailed by scientist and artist alike as an incredible advance toward understanding the essence of movement, a subject that had occupied creative thinkers since Leonardo da Vinci. E. J. Marey had prefaced his work on animal locomotion with the thought, "There is scarcely any branch of animal mechanics which has given rise to more labor and greater controversy than the question of the paces of the horse."[11] A later writer concluded succinctly, "Centuries of eye-straining observation did not permit painters to capture what an instantaneous photograph recorded at Palo Alto Farm."[12]

The scope of the project was enlarged in 1879. The number of cameras was doubled and motion studies were made of a mélange of animals—dogs, cows, oxen, deer, goats. Studies of foreshortening, largely for artistic purposes, were also made. In August the human being was introduced to the arena of study, Stanford inviting a number of athletes to Palo Alto to be photographed.

Muybridge realized that his photographic documents changed widely held notions, both in scientific and artistic circles. Many found it difficult to relinquish their beliefs. Auguste Rodin stated: "It is the artist who is truthful and it is photography which lies, for in reality time does not stop, and if the artist succeeds in producing the impression of a movement which takes several moments for accomplishment, his work is certainly much less conventional than the scientific image, where time is abruptly suspended." But Fairman Rogers, director of the Philadelphia Academy, commented that "Mr. Muybridge deserves the thanks of all artists for the valuable addition that he has made to the general fund of knowledge."

The scientific world hailed the work as an important advance and suggested immediate applications for the singular images of locomotion. Emile Duhousset, author of *Le Cheval*, adapted Muybridge's images to the "philosophical toy," the zoetrope, with good result. The zoetrope, by whatever name, had remained a toy or the tool of a single viewer until an enterprising inventor, A. B. Brown, combined the slotted-disk idea with the magic lantern in 1869 to project the images. Muybridge added one distinctive feature to the mechanism: actual photographs taken of animals in motion. He called his device a zoöpraxiscope and claimed: "It is the first apparatus ever used, or constructed, for synthetically demonstrating movements analytically photographed from life, and in its resulting effects is the prototype of all the various instruments which, under a variety of names, are used for a similar purpose at the present day."[13]

Under Stanford's aegis and approval, he demonstrated the machine in 1879 before a private audience. If his singular images of a horse in motion had aroused keen interest, his reconstruction of action—showing single space-time moments in a continuum—was spectacular. The talented photographer added new dimension to his work when he demonstrated his device and lectured before the public the following year. *Alta California* on 5 May 1880 reported: "Mr. Muybridge has laid the foundation of a new method of entertaining the people, and we predict that his instantaneous photographic, magic-lantern zoetrope will make the rounds of the civilized world."

In 1880 Stanford's patronage for photographic experimentation terminated, although Muybridge continued work at the farm. The following year he presented to his patron a bound album of 203 prints of various subjects in motion. From the standpoint of craftsmanship the album itself was poorly done—the prints crookedly trimmed and mounted. In what it symbolized, however, it was a treasure of which Stanford was justifiably proud. Leland Stanford, a man outside the scientific and artistic circles of London and Paris, had provided the impetus for the experimentation and had used photography as a means toward a specific goal with unbelievable success.

Stanford was persuaded to bring Muybridge and the zoöpraxiscope to Europe. Once there, Muybridge's work caused a sensation, Stanford's contribution all but forgotten beside the power of the photographic image. The camera man captured the stage, charming and awing audiences with his zoöpraxiscope flashing lifesize illusionary motion.

Unfortunately, no written agreements had been made between Muybridge and Stanford concerning the eventual use and ownership of the photographs, and the divergent expectations of each created dissension and finally destroyed the relationship. When Muybridge arrived in Europe in August, 1881, the *British Journal of Photography* ran an advertisement for an edition of *The Attitudes of Animals in Motion* "by Muybridge," with no mention of Stanford, for Muybridge believed the rights to both photographs and negatives were his exclusively. Stanford returned to America shortly thereafter to publish his own volume on *The Horse in Motion* as a scientific study. In the winter of 1880 he had employed his friend Dr. J. D. B. Stillman to begin its preparation, entrusting to the physician the task of analytical interpretation and arrangement of data. When Stanford's book appeared in 1882, its title page bore only the names of Dr. Stillman and Stanford—Muybridge's was conspicuously absent. In the preface, the ex-governor mentioned Muybridge as "a very skillful photographer" whom he had employed. Muybridge, infuriated at being considered a technician, one among many, believed his right to ownership had been violated. Stanford, at the same time, asserted his right to use the photographs as he wished since he had paid for the entire experiment. Muybridge brought suit against his former patron, and the collaborators became antagonists.

The photographer lost his legal battle but emerged the victor, for *The Horse in Motion*, whatever its other faults, lacked the one vital factor that made Stanford's claims unique—the photograph. Stillman included a few reproductions made directly from Muybridge's photographs but relied largely upon drawings to illustrate the book. Whether Stanford and Stillman discounted or disbelieved the impact of the photographic image, the photograph alone—despite its awkward, inelegant black-and-white rendition of reality—for all its primitive, archetypal quality, spoke a truth next to which all else seemed conjecture.

New avenues of photographic endeavor opened to Muybridge and, turning his back on both his former subject matter and the American West, he found a new patron in the East. The University of Pennsylvania offered him an opportunity to expand his photographic studies, and, in 1884, he began an exhaustive study of every conceivable attitude of motion in man and beast, appearing himself in some of the studies as a nude athlete. The work was of interest to art institutions, painters, and students of anatomy and medicine, among others. With that major work completed, he took to the lecture circuit in Europe and America.

With his cameras, Muybridge had penetrated into the heart of motion, stopping it instant by instant to reveal the mechanics of movement, and then he had reconstructed it, synthesizing space-time moments into lifelike activity. He dabbled with his idea of further developing the zoöpraxiscope: "On the 27th of February, 1888, the author, having contemplated some improvements of the zoöpraxiscope, consulted with Mr. Thomas A. Edison as to the practicability of using that instrument in association with the phonograph, so as to combine, and reproduce simultaneously, in the presence of an audience, visible actions and the audible words."[14] But he left the idea of the motion picture to Edison, continuing to lecture on "The Science of Animal Locomotion in its Relation to Design in Art."

In 1893 he opened a Zoöpraxographical Hall at the World's Columbian Exposition in Chicago to lecture and demonstrate before the general public the theories of animal locomotion. Perhaps if he had advertised his hall as "The First Motion Picture House," which in fact it was, he would have played to overflow crowds. As it was, he abandoned the scheme after some months, leaving the development of the motion picture to others.

Instead, he returned to England and began to prepare his work of two decades on locomotion for publication. He published two volumes, one on animal locomotion, the other on human—the summation of his most creative work in photography. With the publication in 1901 of *The Human Figure in Motion*, the septuagenarian retired to Kingston-on-Thames, England. In 1904 death stilled the eccentric man of motion.

Among all the early photographers in the West, Eadweard Muybridge must be reckoned the most worldly and accomplished. He wrote for journals and the publications of his trade, he patented several inventions, he lectured with success to educated audiences, and as a practitioner of the photographic art, he excelled. He rivaled Watkins both in his Yosemite views and in his portfolios of great homes.

Beyond that, Muybridge alone made a significant contribution to the grammar of photography in the nineteenth century, for he expanded and suggested new uses for the medium: first, as a tool of scientific investigation (as opposed to documentation); second, as a medium of motion, producing a forerunner of the moving picture.

It was a rare synchrony that made an aesthete and a railroad baron "co-laborateurs." It could only have happened in the West.

NOTES

1. See Barry B. Combs, *Westward to Promontory* (Palo Alto, Calif.: American West Publishing Co., 1969). In fact, Stanford missed the

spike with the electric wires that would trigger the message, but a quick telegrapher hit the key that would flash the message, "Dot . . . dot . . . dot . . . done."

2. This is the title of the album produced for Stanford. It is described in *Eadweard Muybridge: The Stanford Years, 1872–1882* (Stanford, Calif.: Stanford University Department of Art, 1972), pp. 75–76.

3. *San Francisco Examiner*, 6 February 1881.

4. He wrote home of an interest in photography but no details of the extent or kind. Much of the biographical information is taken from Robert Bartlett Haas, *Muybridge, Man in Motion* (Berkeley: University of California Press, 1976). Haas notes that "five generations of my own family in California have been conservators of original Muybridge materials given by Muybridge himself to my great-grandfather . . . ," and thus his book is an incomparable source of information.

5. *San Francisco Examiner*, 6 February 1881, as cited in *Eadweard Muybridge: The Stanford Years*, p. 119.

6. *Sacramento Union*, 4 February 1875.

7. Brochure advertising Muybridge's 1867 "Yosemite Series," issued by Selleck's Cosmopolitan Gallery of Photographic Art, 1868. California Historical Society, San Francisco.

8. Eadweard J. Muybridge, *Animals in Motion: An Electro-Photographic Investigation of Animal Progressive Movements* (London: Chapman & Hall, 1899), pp. 1–2.

9. Ibid., p. 2.

10. "On Photographing Horses," *British Journal Photographic Almanack* (1872/1873): 115.

11. E. J. Marey, *Animal Mechanism, A Treatise on Terrestrial and Aerial Locomotion* (New York: D. Appleton & Co., 1874), p. 138.

12. An excellent discussion of the artistic and scientific reactions to Muybridge's work is given by Françoise Forster-Hahn, "Marey, Muybridge and Meissonier," *Eadweard Muybridge: The Stanford Years*, pp. 85–109. Unless otherwise noted, the quotations from artists are taken from this volume.

13. Muybridge, *Animals in Motion*, p. 4.

14. Ibid.

37.　THE HIGH SIERRA. 1872

38. FALLS OF THE YOSEMITE. 1872

39.   ATTITUDES OF ANIMALS IN MOTION. HORSES, TROTTING, EDGINGTON, NO. 34. 1879

40.   ATTITUDES OF ANIMALS IN MOTION. HORSES, RUNNING, MAHOMET, NO. 145. 1879

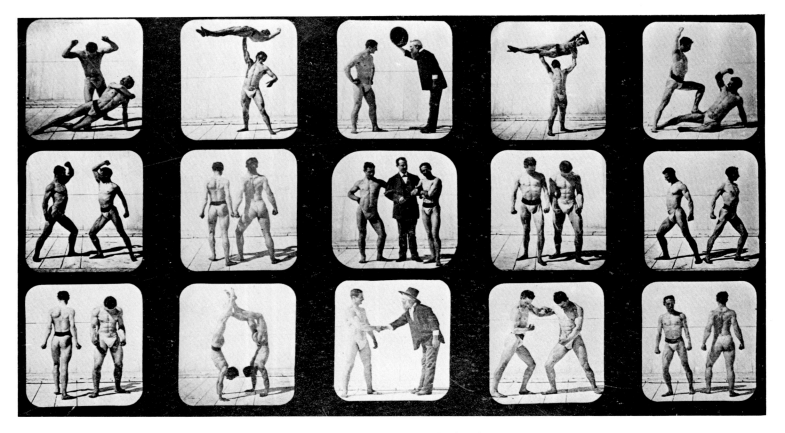

41.   ATTITUDES OF ANIMALS IN MOTION. ATHLETES, CLASSIC GROUPINGS, NO. 116. 1879 [MUYBRIDGE SALUTING ATHLETE]

42. ATTITUDES OF ANIMALS IN MOTION. ATHLETES, SWINGING A PICK, NO. 110. 1879 [ATHLETE IS MUYBRIDGE]

JOHN K. HILLERS
(1843-1925)

"Hillers' buoyant spirit and, at times, ribald sense of humor, endeared him to the Major [John Wesley Powell]. He was the one man who could be breezy and flippant with his chief."[1] Equally hardworking and fun loving, John Hillers became one of the most respected members of the Powell survey, a lifelong friend of Major Powell, and, not incidentally, a photographer whose work is among the finest done by the pioneer photographers of the West.

In his early years in America, this German immigrant neither dreamed of nor sought a career of "shadow-catching." As a young man of eighteen he was swept into the Civil War. After the war he returned to his old neighborhood and joined the Brooklyn Police Force. He might have remained there a lifetime but for an ailing brother who hoped to find health in the West; Jack resigned his police job to accompany him to California. Once there, he obtained work as a teamster, but soon the prospects of sun and silver in Colorado seemed brighter, and the brothers set out for Colorado via Santa Fe, New Mexico.

Major John Wesley Powell altered the plan—and Hillers's life. Overhearing the Major discussing the forthcoming expedition down the Colorado River, Jack knocked on the Major's door and asked for work in order to support his ailing brother. The one-armed Major, a shrewd judge of men, sized him up immediately as stur-dy and fit and hired him as an all-purpose crewman.

Powell had already performed an incredible feat—the descent of the Colorado River from its beginning in Wyoming Territory to its end in eastern Nevada. After that venture, financed with private donations and his own money, he had the admiration of thousands and a Congress willing to appropriate funds.

In truth, few tangible scientific results emerged from his first river reconnaissance—most of the data were forfeited to river rapids or hostile Indians—but it may have been just as well. Encumbered by the huge amount of survival supplies, the scientific apparatus taken along had been minimal. The fact of the journey itself constituted the greatest finding.

The intent of the second exploration was to course the river again in order to achieve a geographical and topographical survey. To this endeavor the Major brought the incalculable benefits of experience and knowledge from the first expedition. He established overland routes to bring fresh supplies along the river route, and concluded agreements with the Indians of the region before starting out.

On 22 May 1871 the second exploration commenced at Green River Station in the Wyoming Territory, but the river had already lost much of its grip on Powell's restless imagination. He was "looking beyond it to the unmapped hinterland, the great problems of physical

43.   POWELL SURVEY. 1879. VIEW IN ZUÑI

geology, most of all the anthropological exhibits, the tribes both extinct and extant that awaited study."[2]

In those first days the party drifted with ease, the Major reading aloud. They stopped along the banks to "geologise," Hillers busying himself with a variety of chores and activities from caulking boats to fishing to singing songs with a good voice and equally good humor.[3] His curiosity soon extended to the photographic image, for Powell had included a photographer named E. O. Beaman on the team. Not long after the journey began, Hillers expressed his interest to Frederick Dellenbaugh, the artist and topographer:

Jack Hillers . . . knew nothing then about photography, but he became much interested as we went on down Green River. . . . Sitting by the fire, Hillers asked me about photography—about the chemical side. I explained about the action of light on a glass plate coated with collodion and sensitized with nitrate of silver, the bath to eliminate the silver in hypo, and so on.

"Why couldn't I do it?" he said. I replied that he certainly could, for he was a careful, cleanly man, and those were the chief qualities needed. I advised him to offer his help to Beaman whenever possible (and aid was then necessary to transport the heavy boxes), and perhaps Beaman would let him try a negative. He did, and in two or three weeks had made such progress that he overshadowed Clement Powell.[4]

Interest and action do not necessarily follow one another, but if there was anything John Hillers was, it was a doer. He established a daily pattern of accompanying the photographic side party, usually composed of the Major, his cousin Clem Powell, and Beaman. More often than not, Hillers carried the heavy equipment. That was his introduction to photography and that was how a boatman entered a new discipline.

Powell's second survey team was well equipped both for the river descent and for measuring data on the plateau areas marked "unexplored" on existing maps. Still, the river ruled—guiding, cajoling, and exacting the same toll of strain, hard work, and physical hardship it had from the first party.

Major Powell led the river exploration only part of the time. Having coursed the waterway once before, he left the party at intervals to study the plateau regions. On October 9 he suddenly announced that the season's river explorations would terminate at the Crossing of the Fathers.

The party wintered at Kanab, Utah, using it as base from which to make reconnaissance trips over the southern regions of Utah. After a few months Major Powell left for Washington, D.C., to gather more appropriations, but before he left he "settled" with the photographer E. O. Beaman. The circumstances involved in the dismissal are not entirely clear, but the parting could hardly be termed friendly. Long before Beaman left the party, Clem Powell (who felt Beaman unwilling to teach him photography) confided to his diary: "Beaman is disliked by all." The consensus was that Beaman was lazy, which may have been true so far as being a member of the team was concerned, but photographically that viewpoint could hardly be supported. Beaman produced more than 130 negatives and several hundred stereos of good technical quality. Many of the party considered Beaman aloof, but Hillers got along very well with him and Beaman taught him a fair amount about the photographic process. Professor Almon Harris Thompson, in general charge of the photographic work, became infuriated when he believed that Beaman had tampered with the chemicals he had left for Clem and ordered payment on Beaman's check stopped. That is also doubtful, for Clem proved totally inept at the process. Privately Beaman wrote to the Major: "As to the charges made against me I have only to say that they are false and were unsuspected by me before my arrival here from the city. Mr. Fennimore [sic] has since worked the bath of which Clement made complaint."[5]

With Beaman gone the position of photographer devolved on the Major's cousin, and Hillers recorded on February 20: "This morning I was installed as assistant photographer." The Shakespeare-reading Clem considered himself a cut above the other men intellectually, but photographically he was a failure. "Clem tried to take some pictures but failed, bath being out of order—fixed it—while manipulating he upset it—so much for the first day," Hillers entered in his diary. Nor did he improve. The wet-plate process simply eluded him, even though Hillers, who already knew a good deal more, offered all manner of help.

Though having shown nepotism in a good many of his appointments, the Major wasted no time in sending to Salt Lake City for a photographer to replace his cousin. Obviously a photographic record of the Grand Canyon journey the following summer could not be sacrificed on the altar of family pride. Within a month James Fennemore, the assistant in the Savage and Ottinger Gallery in Salt Lake, arrived.

Hillers seized the opportunity to learn more about photography. Fennemore was a good photographer and a kindly man, and taught the industrious German all he knew about photography. True, Jack performed many of the laborious chores inherent in photography that one suspects Clem was unwilling to do: "May 5. Washing glass. . . . May 6. Polishing glass. . . . May 7. Cleaning glass." But his willingness and interest earned him the friendship and instruction of "Fen." The pair worked constantly, and Fennemore gave Hillers due credit, listing twenty-seven negatives by "Fennemore and Hillers."[6] At the same time Hillers deferred to Clem, treating the latter's photographic efforts seriously. "Made Clem a dark tent," he recorded on May 21, and later, "Made a ground glass for Clem. . . . Fixed Clem's tripods and camera box."

Under the guidance of Professor Almon Harris Thompson the survey continued to work in a somewhat desultory fashion in anticipation of the Major's arrival. In late June four of the men set out to explore Glen Canyon, Fennemore and Hillers making photographic records of Moqui ruins. Shortly thereafter Hillers recorded: "Fennemore feeling very sick." By mid-August Fen realized that he could not accompany the party through the Grand Canyon, and he took leave of the survey.

It was obvious that Hillers possessed the photographic skill and talent required. He was made photographer-in-chief, and embarked upon a career and a lifetime association with Major Powell.

On 17 August 1872 the party prepared to resume the river voyage near the Crossing of the Fathers, pushing off for Marble Canyon. Rough waters immediately greeted them, and rarely abated. "Continued all day hard at work, making a quarter of a mile," Hillers noted in his diary. After such a day, he undertook his photographic work. He unpacked the equipment and chemicals from their rubber encasements and set up his "crazy old darkroom" of canvas and wood, Beaman having departed with his equipment. Still, Jolly Jack retained the good humor that had earned him his name, and made negatives at every opportunity: "During the day I would take my pictures, and when night came and the boats were tied by the river bank, I would get out my dark-room and chemicals and develop the plates. Sometimes there would be enough light from a wood fire on the bank reflected down to the water to permit me to work. When there was no place to build a fire, someone would hold a lantern back of the light opening, and I would poke my head under the canvas and get to work. I missed a lot of sleep this way."[7]

Forced, as all expeditionary photographers were, to use available water supplies, he would sometimes turn blue from the cold; at other times, "when the water in the Colorado was muddy, we would watch for a clear stream emptying into the river and then get a few bottles of fresh water for some of the finer work."[8] Then he varnished the plates to protect the image until prints could be made.

The river coursed high and incredibly fast, stretching every man's endurance to the limit. The *Emma Dean* capsized, and Hillers and the Major were sucked into a whirlpool. Powell would have lost his life but for Hillers. Less than a week later, the Major terminated the voyage.

Most of the party abandoned the river reconnaissance at that point and headed for Kanab, but Jack and Clem trekked through Kanab Wash to photograph. "Made a picture whenever we found good light on it and sometimes would wait for light. . . . Waited a long time for light—the sun only peeps down into the canon [*sic*] about half an hour, but as the canon [*sic*] changes directions every quarter of a mile, we got good light often. . . . This canon [*sic*] is the most gloomiest place I have ever been in—not a bird in it," wrote Hillers.

With the completion of the river exploration, Hillers came to a definite agreement about his wages with Major Powell, and at the same time an agreement was made concerning the proceeds from the sale of stereos. Powell claimed 40 percent, giving Thompson and Hillers each 30 percent; the Major also claimed the photographers' shares of the Beaman and Fennemore negatives. Such an arrangement hardly seems equitable and, indeed, there was a standing joke at the U.S. Geological Survey in the 1880s that Powell had paid off his Washington, D.C., house mortgage through the sale of these views. It is known that the sales of the first six months of 1874 alone netted him $4,100. Hillers, however, apparently never complained.

In October Jack, Clem, and a guide headed for the mesa country—Hotevilla, Oraibi, Walpi, and Hano—and at the end of November they met William Bell and his assistant with the Wheeler survey. The keen, often bitter rivalry existing among the survey leaders did not influence the respective photographers. Professional interests rather than politics held sway, and they were eager to share their expertise and show their work. Clem Powell recorded: "Bell of Philadelphia and his assistant photographer of Lt. Wheeler's party made us a short visit . . . showed him our negatives. He pronounced them fine. Invited us up to his camp tomorrow to see his negatives." The following day, Hillers and Clem found "Bell and Thompson and others treated us handsomely. Bell showed us how to develop dry plates; do not like the process as well as the wet. Showed us his views; there is too much bare glass to make them first-class. Admired his dark tent and the conveniences he had for taking pictures."[9] Bell's images proved to be very good ones, so apparently Clem's photographic problems were not confined to the process alone.

By 1873, the Major had subtly directed the survey toward his growing interests and had managed to be appointed, along with G. W. Ingalls, as special commissioner for the Indian Bureau. That summer his survey also took on an added dimension as it played host to Thomas Moran. On the first of August, Hillers, Professor Thompson, and Major Powell accompanied Moran to what is now Zion National Park, Hillers being among the first photographers to make images there.[10] Moran commented that "for glory of scenery and stupendous scenic effects," Zion stood alone,[11] the colors dazzling to his painterly vision. They traveled on to Kanab, where Hillers photographed the Paiutes. Here his skill not only as a technician but as an image-maker assumed a larger aspect, for he had an innate feeling for portraiture which

was enhanced and enriched by Moran's eye. Moran posed the subjects in attitudes which the Indians, who trusted Major Powell, assumed. Even though the influence of nineteenth-century art manipulated some of the poses—the Indians were grouped, scattered, dressed, undressed (some with just one breast visible), and redressed, the Major clothing some of the Southern Paiute Indians in buckskin and beaded dresses native to the Northern Utes—they are superb portraits. The combination of art, skill, and trust coming together in the persons of Moran, Hillers, and Powell produced results unequaled by any other early photographer.

"The most valuable ethnographic result of Powell's explorations are the photographs," concluded the eminent ethnologist Julian Steward, regarding the 1873 work.[12] In August, Hillers and Moran moved on toward the Grand Canyon. The route lay parched and scorched, but the grandeur of the canyon dispelled the travail of the journey. Hillers photographed while Moran sat absorbed, making sketch after sketch in his notebooks.

The Major had organized a trip through Kanab Canyon, but the painter's vision had been surfeited. Moran produced illustrations for the popular magazines, however, working from Hillers's fine photographs of Kanab, Glen, and Marble canyons, as well as the inner gorge of the Grand Canyon. For Hillers, the weeks spent in the painter's company were profoundly rewarding to his own seeing and image-making.

Hillers's diary resumed on 1 May 1875 as he prepared to leave on assignment for the Major, to make a series of photographs of the Indian nations in Oklahoma Territory for the Smithsonian Institution and the Bureau of

Indian Affairs display at the Centennial Exposition in Philadelphia. Meeting Ingalls, Hillers undertook the portrayal of the multi-faceted life of the various tribes— Creeks, Seminoles, Cherokees—of the Indian nations. "Here I found six Cheyennes who had just left the war path, all strappen [sic] big fellows. I took them among rocks and set them up as food for my camera. I stripped them to the buff, not a stitch on them except a breach clout and succeeded in making pictures of them all." Portraiture being his special gift, he easily warmed to that aspect of his assignment, but he wrote to the Major he was "tired of photographing churches, school houses and fence rails."[13]

His photographs began to appear in the various survey publications on the Colorado River explorations; in articles that Major Powell wrote for *Scribner's Monthly* and in his book, *Exploration of the Colorado River of the West and Its Tributaries;* and in Clarence Dutton's "Report on the Geology of the High Plateaus of Utah."

In 1879 Powell established the Bureau of Ethnology under the aegis of the Smithsonian Institution and became its first director, appointing Hillers as Bureau photographer. In that position he immediately returned to the Southwest with James Stevenson and Frank Cushing, the team sent to study and photograph the archaeological ruins and the Pueblo Indians. At the same time, although he probably did not realize the full implications, Hillers recorded the demise of many tribal cultures. It was the first of many photographic studies of the Indian that would involve him for the rest of his life. He remained in the employ of John Wesley Powell,

transferring with him to the U.S. Geological Survey when Powell became its director and continuing as chief photographer until 1900.

It seemed unlikely that friendship could exist between two men of such diverse backgrounds and temperaments, but it had been nurtured in difficulties, coursing through rivers and years. Hillers had saved the Major's life, an act which Powell would never forget, and continued to prove himself time and again in countless ways. The friendship ended only with the Major's death in 1902, Hillers serving as pallbearer among an august group of dignitaries.

Hillers continued in the employ of the Bureau of Ethnology on a part-time basis until 1919, during which time he also experimented with techniques and materials for making colored transparencies. Though he never patented his process, he invented a system for coloring glass transparencies that prevented fading.

Jack Hillers learned photography under the most difficult and demanding conditions, helped along the way by those who would share their time and the benefits of their training with an energetic and amiable boatman. In return, he gave a lifetime of government service and fine photographs. On the high plateaus of central and southern Utah he photographed regions rarely if ever before recorded. He was perhaps the first photographer to stand on the rim of the Grand Canyon, as O'Sullivan had penetrated deep within it, to capture a space-time record of the site. His images of the Colorado River explorations provided indisputable witness to those events.

The portfolios Hillers made for the Bureau of Ethnology of the pueblo dwellings along the Rio Grande are remarkable. His photographs show a definite, coherent style, neither haphazard nor accidental. His focus breaks into the architectural gridiron on a diagonal axis, his camera angled so that not only are the architectural ground plan and the elevation of the pueblo shown, but the structure itself also is seen in relationship to the landscape. One view can hardly achieve more.

The images possess clarity and sharpness of detail. In these photographs one is not aware of the limitations that collodion imposed. The monochromatic tones of the pueblo dwellings, indigenous buildings originating from alluvial soil, are well gradated. His views suggest the brilliant quality of New Mexico light—the textures enlivened by it as it reveals the underlying lines and rhythms of the adobe architecture.

Each photograph in the series calculatedly highlights the subtle differences within each pueblo as it settled into its own sympathetic relationship with the land. Hillers alone, of all the early photographers, caught the essence of the contrast between the geometries, a creation of man's mind, and the landscape. Artfully, if instinctively, he placed the Indians among their dwellings to render scale.

To John K. Hillers, as for countless immigrants and settlers alike, the West had offered opportunity and adventure. He had suffered extreme physical exhaustion and incredible hardships to learn photography, but at the end of a hard day he turned his back on them and extracted his due on fragile, glassy surfaces.

Dams have stilled some of the river's wild roaring; roads and fences have invaded regions Hillers was the first to photograph. Spaces have been altered and the silences broken where once he stood alone, waiting for the light to break. But his photographs remain. They are a rich legacy.

NOTES

1. William Culp Darrah, *Powell of the Colorado* (Princeton: Princeton University Press, 1951), p. 212.

2. Wallace Stegner, *Beyond the Hundredth Meridian* (Boston: Houghton Mifflin Co., 1953), p. 137.

3. Almost every member of the survey team began a journal, so a good deal has been revealed about the daily activities. Hillers's diary, little known and eclipsed by the number of accounts by expedition members, remained unpublished for nearly one hundred years. The author was not permitted access to the original Hillers diaries owing to restrictions on the bequest to the Smithsonian Institution; therefore, all references to his diary are taken from an edited source, John K. Hillers, *Photographed All the Best Scenery: Jack Hillers' Diary of the Powell Expeditions, 1871–1875*, ed. Don D. Fowler (Salt Lake City: University of Utah Press, 1972).

4. Dellenbaugh, as quoted in Robert Taft, *Photography and the American Scene* (New York: Macmillan Co., 1938), pp. 289–90.

5. Beaman to Powell, 12 May 1872, Record Group 57, National Archives, Washington, D.C.

6. "Catalog of Negatives, River, Land, and Ethnographic, 1871–1876" (mimeographed), Smithsonian Institution, National Anthropological Archives, Washington, D.C. Fen, as Jack called him, worked for the survey for a few months, producing seventy-one negatives in addition to those he made with Hillers.

7. Hillers, quoted in E. B. Swanson, "Photographing the Grand Canyon Fifty Years Ago," *Mentor* 12 (1924): p. 52.

8. Ibid., pp. 52–53.

9. Charles Kelly, ed., "Journal of W. C. Powell, April 21, 1871–December 7, 1872," *Utah Historical Quarterly* 16–17 (1948–49): pp. 472–73.

10. C. R. Savage early accompanied Brigham Young to Zion, but photographs dated precisely to that trip are not known to exist.

11. Thurman Wilkins, *Thomas Moran: Artist of the Mountains* (Norman, Okla.: University of Oklahoma Press, 1966), p. 58.

12. Julian H. Steward, "Notes on Hillers' Photographs of the Paiute and Ute Indians Taken on the Powell Expedition of 1873," *Smithsonian Miscellaneous Collections*, v. 98, no. 18 (Washington, D.C., 1939). Moran later used several of Hillers's stereos, such as *The Empty Cradle*, as subject matter for his illustrations.

13. Hillers to Powell, 2 June 1875, Record Group 57, National Archives, Washington, D.C.

44. POWELL SURVEY. 1879. GOVERNORS OF ZUÑI

45.   POWELL SURVEY. 1879. CAPTAINS OF THE CANYON DE CHELLY

46.   POWELL SURVEY. 1879. SANTO DOMINGO, NEW MEXICO

47. INQUIRING FOR THE WATER POCKET. ON HORSE: MAJOR JOHN W. POWELL. 1871

48. MA-NU-NI, ALL OF THE TRIBE; WITH MORMON AND GENTILE SPECTATORS

49.   POWELL SURVEY. 1879. ZUÑI, LOOKING SOUTHEAST

50. INDIAN BOY AND HIS DOG; UINTA UTES LIVING IN THE
UINTA VALLEY ON THE WESTERN SLOPE OF THE WASATCH
MOUNTAINS, UTAH

51. THE BASKET MAKER. KAI-VAV-ITS

52. PILE OF LITTLE INDIANS. KAI-VAV-ITS. A TRIBE OF THE PAIUTES LIVING ON THE KAIBAB PLATEAU NEAR THE GRAND CANYON OF THE COLORADO IN NORTHERN ARIZONA

53. THE WARRIOR AND HIS BRIDE; UINTA UTES

WILLIAM HENRY JACKSON
(1843-1942)

Born just four years after Daguerre had fixed that first fragile image, William Henry Jackson's life spanned nearly the first hundred years of photography. He lived to see photographic apparatus, once measured in hundreds of pounds and carried by mules, shrink to pocket-size maneuverability, and the image evolve into a full range of grays and even into color.

For every spare word attributed to Timothy O'Sullivan, William Jackson left thousands; this, and an abundance of articles and publications by others, leaves little unknown about his long career. But to assess the significance to photography and the impact of this enormously productive man, who made tens of thousands of negatives, is equally as difficult to decipher from the deluge of existing facts and opinions, and extant prints.

Jackson dated his photographic beginnings to childhood, claiming that his father had begun experimenting with a camera when the daguerreotype first appeared.[1] His mother, an able watercolorist, gave William the *American Book of Drawing*, from which many an early illustrator learned the basics. If young William was not overly talented, as his drawings reveal, he nevertheless enjoyed himself and pursued the discipline with energy and unselfconscious enthusiasm. This attitude prevailed in various activities throughout his life and contributed largely to his success.

Jackson worked from the time he was twelve until he was ninety-nine. Age fourteen found him in the first of countless photographic studios he would eventually occupy. He had yet to operate a camera, but by about 1860, when he moved to Rutland, Vermont, and a better position, he knew a fair amount about photography.

Enlistment in the army during the Civil War only briefly interrupted his career and in fact offered Jackson further opportunity to pursue his interests. He breezed through his stint in the army, seeing neither combat nor any of Brady's photographic teams. At the outset he was stationed near Washington, D.C., thus enabling him to seek out the art in the Capitol and the Smithsonian, and his single year of army service as staff artist was spent making sketches of the countryside to aid in mapping the area. He had plenty of time to fill his own sketchbook and notebook, and even earned a little extra money making portraits of soldiers. Upon mustering out he found a position in a larger gallery but soon, at age twenty-three, he was bullwhacking his way to the land of golden promise, California. The promise never materialized, however, and in May, 1867, he decided to return East by working his way as a driver of wild horses. "Mustang Jack" planted his feet in Omaha in August, 1867, and gladly exchanged his dreams of silver mining for a steady job in a photographic gallery.

Less than a year later the enterprising Jackson made a small down payment on the business and, with his

54. THE BEEHIVE GROUP OF GEYSERS, YELLOWSTONE PARK

brother Edward, "Jackson Brothers, Photographers" became a thriving and profitable portrait gallery. "Although my business lay properly with the pallet and brush, I could not resist the temptation to dabble among the chemicals," he wrote a few years later. "Portrait photography never had any charms for me, so I sought my subjects from the house-tops, and finally from the hill-tops and about the surrounding country; the taste strengthening as my successes became greater in proportion to the failures." He outfitted a wagon, but "in the one or two trips made with it, I was so invariably mistaken for an itinerant showman, that I got disgusted with it."[2] He did make photographs of Plains Indians, many of them the first portraits made.

The railway put Jackson on the move, giving him easy access to a region rich in interest. With an assistant named Arundel C. Hull he headed for Cheyenne, making pictures of the scenic and picturesque effects along the Union Pacific route, riding the rails of speculation to establish his reputation. Loaded with one hundred 8-by-10 and two hundred stereo plates, the pair traveled from station to station.

The most important result of that summer of travel was that his images caught the interest of Ferdinand Vandiveer Hayden, who would loom large in Jackson's future. Hayden was looking for a photographer to accompany his next expedition, and Jackson was invited to join Hayden's survey in July, 1870, though without salary. Hayden did, however, give Jackson the right to all negatives for his own use, unlike Powell, who took the largest percentage from the sale of stereo views made by his photographers. Jackson, always adept at recognizing opportunity and never one to deny challenge, quickly signed on and reported to Hayden the first week in August.

The 1870 explorations centered in territory largely familiar to Hayden. Jackson had also been over part of the trail—first as bullwhacker, then as vaquero, finally as commercial photographer—but he made hundreds of photographs that first season, working with a 6-by-8 instrument that also could be used for stereo views. He photographed from the 12,000-foot peaks in the Uintas, where melted snow washed his plates, to the deep canyons of the Green River, packing his mule "Hypo" to reach more out-of-the-way points. The group headed across Wyoming somewhat north of the Union Pacific Railroad. From their western terminus, Fort Bridger, where the Mormon and Oregon trails divided, they turned south, exploring among the Uinta Mountains. They followed Henry's Fork to its juncture with the Green River, then journeyed along the Green through deepening canyons until they reached Brown's Hole. They then worked their way to Cheyenne, where they arrived on the first of November.

Jackson received an official appointment as a salaried photographer that lasted the duration of Hayden's survey. The first season they roamed the familiar, but during the second they explored the fantastic: Yellowstone. The area was not entirely unknown, but many thought it was more the creation of facile storytellers than of nature. Hayden, having long desired to explore it, convinced Congress that he was just the man to conduct a scientific exploration. With his $40,000 appropriation he assembled a large party, including Thomas Moran, who, though slight of frame, proved to be a sizable presence.

A close affinity developed between the two image-makers, Moran and Jackson. They kept practically constant company, making junkets apart from the main group, Jackson with his camera-laden mule and Moran with his sketchbook. The painter appears in many of Jackson's views—as an evocative silhouette fishing on Yellowstone Lake or as an inquiring bowler-hatted tourist amid the crystalline structures. Moran became greatly interested in photography, and helped Jackson solve many problems of composition. It was Moran, in fact, who scouted out views in advance, both for sketches and photographs, his artistry aiding in the selection of the photographic representations that Jackson produced. With Moran's assistance, Jackson was able to produce up to twenty negatives a day with his 8-by-10 camera, as well as stereo views. They moved from one marvelous place to another, from Tower Falls to Mount Washburn to the Grand Canyon of the Yellowstone, lingering here, drifting afield there. On their way out of the Yellowstone country a last marvel awaited them—the geysers of Firehole Basin, where both men made their final images.

Moran left the survey at this point to hurry East with his sketches, anxious to translate the total experience into final form, but Jackson finished the season's work with the survey. Moran produced a series of sketches and watercolors for several publications, and Jackson worked long hours to print his negatives. Within months

both had produced substantial evidence of the once-mythical realm of Yellowstone: Jackson's photographs confirmed the reality of its existence, documenting the bizarre formations and natural wonders; Moran's watercolors evoked the beauty of the region, moving everyone who saw his fantastic colorations. Description might exaggerate, but the camera told the truth. Others had suggested that Yellowstone should be preserved, but now Hayden became the outspoken advocate, his argument supported by two compelling testimonials: Moran's illustrations and Jackson's album titled *Yellowstone's Scenic Wonders*. Yellowstone became the first national park in America in March, 1872.

Yellowstone was the making of both these artists' reputations. Through a series of fortunate circumstances, Jackson's photographs became the first to be published. Another photographer, Thomas J. Hines, had been traveling with Captain J. W. Barlow's party of engineer-explorers concurrent with Hayden's expedition, and had returned home to print his negatives, only to arrive on the eve of the Chicago fire; almost every negative was destroyed. A local photographer named J. Crissman had accompanied the expedition unofficially and met with limited success (at one point his entire outfit was blown over the canyon rim, but Jackson lent him an extra). In any event, Crissman's photographs reached only a local market while Jackson's were distributed to members of Congress, and were widely disseminated. The next season's survey found Hayden's party even larger. Jackson now commanded an independent photographic unit of five men, and he added an 11-by-14 camera, with accompanying equipment, to his already hefty outfit. Heading for Teton Range with James Stevenson's contingent, the photographic unit tramped to the crest of the western wall of the gorge where Jackson photographed the Grand Teton, which rises nearly 14,000 feet. They rendezvoused with the Hayden detachment at the Firehole Basin in Yellowstone in mid-August, and the group headed north along the Gallatin River on their way home. Even though a disgruntled mule jettisoned a load of photographic material into the river, Jackson again came away with a good season's work. The party disbanded and Jackson returned to Omaha to sell his studio, having decided to move to Washington, D.C.

The next year brought a vigorous season in mountain peaks, largely in Colorado. Jackson again headed an independent group, and this time he attempted panoramic views that swept from peak to peak, encompassing distances of up to one hundred miles, by taking a series of images that he then fitted together.

Photographing in such a landscape was fraught with problems, and one of the mules added to the difficulties when he tumbled down the hill and broke a number of negatives. Undaunted, Jackson returned and re-took the views; he was in his element.

During the summer, in the region of Twin Lakes, the Hayden party encountered one of the Wheeler survey groups. "Thus the absurd spectacle presented itself of two surveying parties, their instruments placed on the same remote mountain peaks, surveying the same wilderness territory."[3] (Clarence King, too, had already explored part of the region that Hayden surveyed, notably

the Uintas.) If Hayden and Wheeler were less than thrilled at the encounter, their respective photographers, Jackson and O'Sullivan, welcomed the opportunity to share field notes and reportedly traded negatives of the area to aid each other.

For Jackson the most important subject matter of the season lay ahead, where—legends told—a mysterious mountain stood, with an eternally snow-filled cross near its summit. As a scientific objective, the quest to find the mountain was doubtful, but Hayden's revelations of natural wonders enhanced his public image, even if other survey leaders were critical.

In search of the holy mountain, the party followed the general guidelines and advice of the wilderness men who claimed to have seen it. Two days of arduous climbing over a trail strewn with fallen timber and willow thickets brought them near their goal. Then the rarefied atmosphere forced the animals to a halt, and Jackson and his two assistants packed a hundred pounds of cameras, plate boxes, and chemicals on their backs and struggled to the crest of Notch Mountain. Clouds covered the peak, so the group huddled through the cold night awaiting the clear light of dawn; then they climbed to the summit. The cross was there, and Jackson became the first man to photograph it, using each of his cameras, the stereo and the 11-by-14. The experience was sublime: "I have never come close to matching those first plates," he confided years later.

Jackson enjoyed a wide reputation based on his Yellowstone images, but his photographs of the Mount of the Holy Cross brought him recognition from every quarter of society. Thomas Moran, inspired by the subject documented in Jackson's photographs, made a journey West to see the cross for himself and used it as the theme of one of his greatest paintings. Henry Wadsworth Longfellow, moved by the natural symbol, wrote of the cross on the mountain as an equivalent to the cross he bore over his wife's death. Untold numbers of Americans gazed upon Jackson's prints of the cross at the 1876 Centennial Exposition in Philadelphia and accolades and medals were heaped upon him.

Jackson's fame, had he never made another image, would have been secure, but he was to be the first to witness yet another significant discovery the following year. The survey got a late start in July. Jackson headed toward the San Juan Mountains and the mesa country to the south. Feeling hurried by the lateness of the season, he took only his 5-by-8 camera, which he also used for stereo views. He stopped to photograph Harry Yount, first ranger of Yellowstone National Park, atop Berthoud Pass, and pushed on to the Los Piños Agency to photograph the Ute Indians. He made a portrait of Chief Ouray, but generally the Utes regarded the white man with suspicion and the camera as bad medicine, so Jackson moved on, finding more mountain peaks to satisfy his quest for high places.

The find of the season awaited in mesa country. Jackson learned of a man who claimed the existence of cliff cities in the canyons of the Mesa Verde. It intrigued Jackson, who never turned down the promise of novel photographic subject matter, and a correspondent named Ernest Ingersoll, who had joined him, sensed that the real story might be there. In late September they went in search of forgotten cities, guided by Captain John Moss. They journeyed into the valleys, the canyon walls closing in as daylight—and enthusiasm—began to fade. Evidence of previous habitation existed, but nothing really grand or picturesque, and the party began to feel a bit discouraged. Then, in the cleft of the rock face, a two-story dwelling of long-vanished cliff builders revealed itself. Unable to wait, Jackson and Ingersoll worked their way upward using the ancient toeholds. It was true. The following morning they hauled the camera up the side of the canyon and Jackson's lens focused again on unique subject matter—the prehistoric Indian dwellings in Mesa Verde.

Exhilarated by the find, they hurried on into the valley, siting ruins on every side. Had they paused to explore some of the side canyons not far from that first discovery, they would have been dazzled by the most spectacular dwelling of all—the Cliff Palace. But no matter—W. H. Jackson had done it again.

In June, 1875, he set out through the Rocky Mountains once more, this time in the company of William Holmes. He was carrying the largest camera he had ever used, a gigantic 20-by-24, but Jackson scouted his pictures with a smaller camera first.

They covered the San Juan area and Hovenweep, then moved on to Canyon de Chelly, where Timothy O'Sullivan had stood with his camera only a few years before. Holmes made careful notes and drawings of the strange beasts and images carved into the rocks by the ancients, and Jackson, too, made notes. Their trip encompassed the ruins of Chaco Canyon, Pueblo Pintado, and the villages of the Hopi, atop Arizona mesas. In many of these areas they were certainly not the first white visitors, "but their reports, including diagrams, sketches, illustrations of pottery, and precise descriptions, constituted a landmark in the history of Southwestern archaeology."[4]

Back in Washington, Jackson began to organize the survey's portion of the Department of the Interior exhibition for the 1876 Centennial Exposition, and he stayed with the exhibit the following year.

Anxious to return to the field, Jackson again wanted to visit the mesa country. With Hayden's approval he left the main survey party and traveled with a friend, though it meant photographing without benefit of packers and assistants. Because of that, Jackson decided to try a new dry-base film called "Sensitive Negative Tissue," which he had seen advertised in an English photographic journal. It came packed in rolls sufficient for twenty-four 8-by-10 exposures, and the prospect of such an easy and portable material, as well as the advantage of not having to find water in semi-arid conditions in which to develop films sounded ideal. Unfortunately, Jackson's enthusiasm overcame discretion. He performed only a quick test, the tissue arriving late, and set off for the Southwest. He exposed hundreds of feet of film, waiting till the end of the season to develop them in Washington. Not one image returned with him, apparently because of the delay in developing. Nonetheless, the trip had yielded important archaeological discoveries in Chaco Canyon, which Jackson described in his "Report on the Ancient Ruins Examined in 1874–1875 and 1877."

Machinations in Washington, maneuverings among the principal survey leaders, and a Congress irritated by the duplications in survey explorations made the 1878 Hayden survey the final one. Hayden returned to the field of his 1871–72 explorations in the Tetons, Yellowstone, and the Wind River Mountains. Jackson took his 5-by-8 and his 11-by-14 cameras, and he used the new, dry collodion-bromide plates. These were commercially available but the chemicals seemed unusually erratic. Though the last trip was not too productive, the survey years overall proved unbelievably successful: "I had established myself as one of the foremost landscape photographers in the country. My career was assured. I loved my work."[5]

His government service concluded, Jackson moved to Denver and opened a studio in 1879, styling himself a "commercial landscape photographer." For most of the next two decades he continued to seek out and create opportunities to make a living with his camera, and to record the "incomparable beauties, grandeurs, and marvellous wonders," particularly in America. Jackson's ambitious and adventurous lens would look all over—within the country and out, to nearby Mexico and faraway Siberia—and retrace favored viewing places to make salable pictures. He would experiment with new techniques and, with indefatigable enthusiasm, accept assignments as diversified as photographing the World's Columbian Exposition in Chicago in 1893 to embarking on a trip around the world with the World Transportation Commission.

W. H. Jackson compiled an enormous body of work, particularly of western subjects. When the Kodak was first introduced, he simply channeled his photographic endeavors in new directions. He allied himself with the Detroit Publishing Company, which turned thousands of his images into tinted postcards and hand-colored photographs, and he made new views for the firm. At the same time, "an important purpose of Jackson's travels was to make contact with local photographers who might do work for the company and on occasion to purchase existing files of negatives. Efforts to . . . ascertain the names of collections absorbed by the company have so far eluded research."[6] Jackson himself did not label the work of other photographers and when he died, leaving upwards of fifty thousand negatives and untold numbers of prints, he took the knowledge of their sources with him. Some of the work in the collection is identifiable—the Indian images of several photographers, such as Alexander Gardner, John Hillers, Ben Wittick, and Adam Vroman; other work, because it differs greatly from Jackson's style, is known only *not* to be his.

A better camera explorer could not have been found if Hayden had had to invent one. In William Henry Jackson he chanced upon a hardy, intrepid photographer whose drive pushed the medium—and the man himself —into unknown and uncharted areas. He loved vast spaces and high mountains, and he never lost the capacity to be astonished.

Photographically, his approach was neither inventive nor interpretive but direct. In attempting to produce as many views as possible, with an eye to their commercial potential as well, he snapped every aspect of a landscape in a given place as time and light would allow. The net result is quantities of largely haphazard pictures. Yet he was precisely the kind of pioneer picture-maker the West needed. He photographed the land as he found it, and time and again he was the first one there. Even a century later, his singular images are of value from many standpoints. They remain the earliest benchmark against which change—geological, ecological, botanical—can be measured.

Some of his photographs of high places—where clouds, wind, and lightning are as vital to the landscape as the substantive elements—seem cold, bordering on the indifferent because they are devoid of atmosphere. Unlike O'Sullivan's images, in which the blank sky strengthens the view, Jackson's suffered. Years later, remembering a mountain landscape, Jackson lamented, "Oh, that I had had a Kodak, by means of which such passing effects could have been instantly secured!"[7] But he photographed as best he could and with enormous energy, self-confident enthusiasm, and competent technique.

NOTES

1. William H. Jackson, in collaboration with Howard R. Driggs, *The Pioneer Photographer* (Yonkers, New York: World Book Co., 1929), p. 1.

2. William H. Jackson, "Field Work," *Philadelphia Photographer* 12 (1875): 91.

3. William H. Goetzmann, *Exploration and Empire* (New York: Alfred A. Knopf, 1966), p. 478.

4. Ibid., p. 525.

5. Jackson, *Time Exposure* (New York: G. P. Putnam's Sons, 1940), p. 251.

6. Paul Vanderbilt, comp., *Guide to the Special Collections of Prints and Photographs in the Library of Congress* (Washington, D.C.: Government Printing Office, 1955), p. 48.

7. Jackson, *The Pioneer Photographer*, p. 212.

55. HIGH BRIDGE AT THE "LOOP" ABOVE GEORGETOWN, COLORADO CENTRAL RAILWAY

56. TOWER FALLS

57. EMBUDO, NEW MEXICO

58.   HERCULES' PILLARS, COLUMBIA RIVER, OREGON

59.   PALACE BUTTE PARK, GALLATIN MOUNTAINS, MONTANA TERRITORY

60.   MYSTIC LAKE, MONTANA TERRITORY

61.   DEVIL'S SLIDE, WEBER CANYON, UTAH

62.   RAINBOW FALLS, WINTER

63. CLIFF PALACE, MESA VERDE

64.   NEAR SAPINERO, ENTRANCE TO THE BLACK CANYON

65. THOMAS MORAN FISHING, YELLOWSTONE LAKE ("FISH POT," HOT SPRINGS, YELLOWSTONE LAKE)

66. CHALK CREEK CANYON

67.   ST. PETER'S DOME. SHORT LINE, COLORADO SOUTHERN AND COLORADO CENTRAL LINE

68.   Solomon D. Butcher, W. H. BLAIR OF HUCKLEBERRY, NEAR BROKEN BOW, NEBRASKA. 1888, DETAIL

The Settling Years

"The federal government, like a mother, had created the West—first by fighting wars of expansion and then by parceling out the public domain. Thereafter the federal government nourished and protected the area through army exploration, subsidies for transportation, encouragement of settlement, and the general promotion of economic development."[1]

Photography witnessed the creation of the West, and from the moment of its birth faithfully recorded and documented it in all its many facets. A thousand miles and undreamed natural wonders away, even as photography took to the field on the great explorations in the post-Civil War years, the camera stood a ready witness.

Congress had dangled the bait of free land before settler and railway builder with the 1862 Homestead Act and the Pacific Railroad Bill. Actual construction of a transcontinental railroad proved to require far larger inducements, however, and by 1866 the Union Pacific had progressed a mere 250 miles west of Omaha. Still, it occasioned a celebration, for the tracks represented tangible evidence that the Northwest Passage—the long-dreamed-of route to India—was at long last a possibility.

By the next year the building of the railway had gathered momentum as the big companies rushed to devour the incentives of more money and more land. Four hundred rails to the mile, five men to a five-hundred-pound rail, over seemingly endless prairie grass and into the hearts of mountains and out again, the iron snake followed its continental course.

Photographers chronicled the phenomenal endeavor. Captain Andrew J. Russell followed the Union Pacific in its westward marathon and Alfred A. Hart accompanied the Central Pacific race to the East. In May, 1869, the engines stood waiting for the golden spike to join East and West. Three photographers (Charles R. Savage of Salt Lake City was the third) set up their cameras at Promontory Point to record the historic occasion when the "flax" of steel rails would be transformed into a single transcontinental thread of "gold"; it seemed as magical as the maiden's spinning for Rumpelstiltskin, and produced equally immediate results. Unbelievable expansion and exploitation followed. The trains fed the West with an ever-increasing land-hungry population and with seekers of opportunity, numerous cameramen among them. The ranks of professional photographers doubled, surpassing 7,500 in number. It was not that the wet-plate collodion process had become easier, it was simply that the West—and opportunity—had become more accessible.

Studios blossomed in every town, and from his established place of business an enterprising photographer could journey short distances to record the drama of the settling experience, with its lively cast of characters, many of whom would become legendary in their own time. If a cameraman could not yet capture the immediacy of the moment, he could at least arrest some of its textures and patterns and the people involved.

An infinite variety of lucrative and exotic subject matter was available. There was the land itself, full of curiosities and wonders; the people—the settlers, cowboys and Indians, and the military; the man-made forms interjecting their designs onto the contours of that vast stretch of the continent—from Montana to Texas, Kansas to California—known simply as the West. As never before, the taming and civilizing of a land flickered before countless camera lenses.

The war for the Plains between Indian and white man had begun in the early 1860s, but the government's attention was temporarily diverted by the larger conflict of the Civil War. In the postwar period, however, all eyes were focused on the Indian's claim to the land, and with near unanimity it was agreed he had none. The Indian understood all too well that the coming of a railroad would alter his way of life, and had vainly sought to discourage survey parties. Once the railroads followed the trackings of the surveyors, however, the Indian could do precious little. Almost as soon as the railroads planted their iron feet upon the soil, they spawned a cattle empire—for they connected beef to eastern appetites and what was an enormous market. By 1868 the Loving-Goodnight Trail stretched all the way to Cheyenne, and in three years the Chisholm Trail had deposited more than a million cattle in Abilene, Kansas. As the cattle empire expanded, the buffalo herds correspondingly contracted (they were being hunted by the white man as well). His source of sustenance diminished, the Indian himself was herded into smaller and smaller islands of space by the military.

Many an enterprising photographer sought to capture on glass the fugitive spectacle that passed before his lens.

Will Soule photographed the Indians on his own, working first as a clerk at Fort Dodge, Kansas, and later as post photographer at Fort Sill, Indian Territory (Oklahoma), in the years 1867–74. L. A. Huffman arrived at Fort Keogh, Montana Territory, in 1878, in time to photograph the "pacified" but not yet defeated Sioux.

The 1870s were the golden age of Indian photography, and produced some of the most valuable historical and ethnological documentation. Within a decade, a way of life had vanished and the opportunity to photograph "wild Indians" with it, except for the wily Geronimo and his Apache band, who managed to elude capture for a few brief years.

Photographically speaking, 1878 marked the beginning of the second revolution in the medium, for a New York manufacturer, Albert Levy, began production of gelatin dry plates for the American market. Thereafter photography, in essence, assumed a distinctly different—and modern—character. The implications reached far beyond the obvious changes and resulting ease in the photographic process; they touched upon the very nature of, and beliefs about, the medium itself: if collodion had placed the photographic *image* within the reach of nearly every person, the dry plate put a camera in his hand. Still, photography was not as simple as the promotional claims of manufacturers suggested. Certain optical and chemical principles had to be grasped, such as the relationship of the lens aperture to light rays, and the chemistries involved in developing negatives. "Instantaneous" in fact translated into 1/25 second exposure, under optimum conditions. And it must be remembered that the manufacturers themselves promised only that the dry plate would produce "presentable" pictures, not fine ones.

The gelatin dry plate bore the same relationship to the photographer as tube paint to the artist—both allowed the user to work in natural surroundings to capture something of the instantaneous quality of a scene. In contrast to the collodionized wet plate, the dry plate offered varying grain sizes, making a wider range of speeds available, and required only one-tenth to one-twentieth the exposure of the wet plate. Relatively speaking, it made instantaneous and action shots possible. It also rendered a substantially longer tonal range, because gelatin acted as a mask for unexposed silver during developing. And it reduced the massive amount of equipment necessary, eliminating the traveling darkroom with its trays and bottles. Cameras, though by no means lightweight, could be hand held.

Preparation of the gelatin formulas was considerably more complex than that of the collodion mixtures, which had allowed a fair amount of latitude, and it placed the dry plate beyond the expertise of the photographer.

The dry plate also took the manufacture of photographic equipment out of the how-to-do-it realm and placed it firmly into industrial mass production. The obvious corollary to standardized, uniform dry plates was a camera with a format that matched, and the increased sensitivity of the dry plate necessitated stricter standards —light-tight cameras, bellows, and holders, and reasonably accurate shutter mechanisms.

At the same time the kind of practitioner that the dry plate attracted to photography differed markedly from that of the collodion era. The collodion wet-plate process had demanded a certain amount of chemical aptitude and mechanical ability, with a liberal dash of ingenuity, particularly in the field; the dry-plate technique devolved to following the instructions implicitly. The stimulus to experiment and devise one's own methods was supplanted by the claim that with the dry plate, "no previous knowledge of photography is required." While the number of professional photographers doubled in the decade of the 1880s, photography as a popular pastime became a mass movement.

The first revolution in photography—from daguerreotypy to wet-plate collodion—brought forth the paper print, filling drawing-room walls, frames, albums, and stereoscopes. It made the photograph a highly popular commercial item that countless Americans could afford, in some form or another. Photography itself, however, still retained a certain mystique; the camera operator seemed something of a magician, shrouded as he was under his dark cloth, and the process of making and transmuting the latent image into a positive held a bit of mystery. The second revolution—from wet plate to dry —threatened to depose both the professional photographer and photography from their privileged position. It had happened before photographers had caught their breath, so to speak—less than fifty years since the daguerreotypist first inhaled the heady fumes of mercury as he produced the precious silver image. While for years photographers had clamored for faster emulsions to stop motion and capture atmospheric conditions, more than a few professional photographers were convinced that, with the dry plate and the hand camera, science had opened a Pandora's box. They could try to resist, but the amateur market offered an incalculable number of enthusiasts and a portent of the future. As the dry plate gained in reputation, the market gathered momentum and manufacturers were able to reduce substantially the costs of production—initially a large barrier to acceptance. The do-it-yourselfers swarmed to the gelatin like bears to honey.

The cameramen of the West welcomed the revolution that the dry plate wrought in the medium—it made one task easier in a place and time when little else was—and they were the first to acknowledge the advantages the new technology offered.

Established photographers in the East (though San Franciscan Carleton Watkins and others were also affected) worried about the rising ranks of amateurs, concerned that they would usurp their business. Many began to try to produce "artistic" portraits, which often meant elaborate backdrops and retouching, to distinguish their work from that of the new practitioners. Mass production had taken photography over before an art tradition within it had gained tentative footing in America.

The imagist of the West had few artistic concerns. For almost any camera operator the West offered plenty of space to practice and no lack of clients. The places, people, and events filled his lens with sufficient novelty and wonder to make such pretensions superfluous. Many photographers who documented the settling experience did, in fact, develop a very good sense of composition and a definable style, but it seems to have evolved out of innate sensitivity, such as George Edward Anderson possessed, or from the subject matter itself, as was the case with Solomon Butcher.

Photography as an amateur enterprise was not common in the West in the settling years. Where life was difficult and survival the overriding concern, such pursuits remained peripheral. Then, too, photography was comparatively costly, particularly to those struggling to sustain existence with the resources at hand. Photographers held few illusions that they would get rich in the business—many accepted whatever goods in payment a struggling customer could offer—but there was a living to be made for those who were enterprising and willing to produce everything from an inexpensive tintype to a stereo view.

In truth, it could be said that the instantaneous dry plate arrived not a moment too soon on the western front—for the frontier was as much an event as a place, a passing phenomenon that might have been "a dream and a forgetting."

NOTES

1. Robert V. Hine, *The American West: An Interpretive History* (Boston: Little, Brown and Co., 1973), p. 281.

BUILDING THE RAILROAD:
ANDREW J. RUSSELL (1830–1902)

If Captain Andrew J. Russell himself had composed the job description for the photographic position available with the Union Pacific Railroad, it could not have matched his qualifications more perfectly. The task the Union Pacific had in mind was the photographic documentation of the event of the age—the building of the transcontinental railroad—with an eye to attracting investors, settlers, and tourists. To that assignment Russell brought an impressive array of talent and experience.

Before he entered the Civil War, Andrew Russell already was an experienced photographer with a studio background and an awareness of the photography of the period.[1] Russell learned field photography in the difficult arena of war, although he never faced battle conditions with his camera as Mathew Brady's men did. A throughly competent technician, Russell seems to have held one of the most important photographic positions in the military. He had been detached to photograph construction and fortifications for the United States Military Railroad Construction Corps, an assignment he held throughout the war. Neither was Russell an ordinary enlistee. He had entered with, or achieved, the rank of captain in the infantry. It was not a difficult transition, then, to become a company man and to work under the command of a young major general, Grenville Dodge, who was chief engineer for the Union Pacific Railroad.

Russell also had artistic training. He had been a teacher of penmanship in upstate New York, and he practiced both photography and painting during the war. How proficient he was in both these arts can only be conjectured, but photographic evidence suggests he possessed a keen sense of composition.

The photographic commission from the Union Pacific Railroad—to follow the track over an already surveyed route—differed greatly from commissions to photograph government surveys. Survey photographers never knew from one day to the next what to expect, while Russell's subject matter was well defined in advance, the railroad officials holding preconceived notions of what would be useful. Though an element of the unknown existed, unexpected encounters were largely eliminated from the company's plan, which was to establish the straightest line practicable on the flattest bed possible.

By fall of 1866 the rails had reached the Hundredth Meridian, barely 250 miles from civilization. Winter of the following year found the Union Pacific crew at Cheyenne, having tracked 450 miles from Omaha. The right moment for a vigorous promotion campaign had arrived, now that part of the transcontinental link was a steel fact.

By early 1868 Russell had been engaged to produce a visual document which was "calculated to interest all classes of people, and to excite the admiration of all reflecting minds as the colossal grandeur of the Agricul-

69. EAST AND WEST SHAKING HANDS. MAY 10, 1869

tural, Mineral and Commercial resources of the West are brought to view."[2]

Once hired, Russell and his photographic team hurried to Cheyenne, but the construction crew had already taken off at breakneck speed. The photographic team caught up but had to keep up, and Russell needed all his considerable skill to meet the conditions that the assignment and the West imposed. He learned to work quickly and to take everything as it came, which often meant that the traveling darkroom appeared in the pictures; more than once the trash and mess of hurried construction was strewn in the foreground of his photographs. He also brought his Yankee ingenuity to bear. He devised a camera with two distinct refinements and published the design, which he claimed was more "compact, durable, light and convenient and far from being complicated in its construction."[3] He designed a focus scale on the rail of the base of the camera box so that the lens could be moved quickly to a prejudged footage, which greatly speeded the focusing process. His second improvement, aside from lighter construction, which eased the camera's ungainliness, was whalebone corners on the plateholders, making them impervious to acid and silver.

The men and the construction stopped only momentarily. An eastern newsman described the incredible pace: "A light car, drawn by a single horse, gallops up to the front with its load of rails. Two men seize the end of a rail and start forward, the rest of the gang taking hold by twos, until it is clear of the car. They come forward at a run. At the word of command the rail is dropped in its place, right side up with care, while the same process goes on at the other side of the car. Less than thirty seconds to a rail for each gang, and so four rails go down to the minute. . . . Close behind the first gang come the gaugers, spikers, and bolters, and a lively time they make of it. It is a grand 'anvil' chorus."[4]

The conditions under which the construction crews worked were unbelievable. Food, consisting largely of beef, bread, and black coffee, was served on plates that were nailed to the table. When one contingent of the crew had bolted their ration the tables were swabbed with buckets of water, and the next shift sat down.

Though Captain Russell no doubt lived a bit better than the Irish immigrant laborers, he still had to be tough to survive the rigors and the pace. And not only did he have to get along with the men, he had to exercise a certain amount of authority in order to procure the carefully posed images he wanted. It is evident from the photographs he made of the diverse group members that he succeeded. He photographed the anonymous laborers against the backdrop of the harsh landscape and the brutal machinery, and captured them looking challengingly and directly into the camera. He caught the essence of General Jack Casement, who seemed to the rough workers he bossed "seven feet tall and tough as nails,"[5] though in fact he stood barely five feet tall. Russell posed him with Cossack cap and bull whip, striding alone alongside the track with the crew looking on, the angle of view heightening the psychological stature of the man who embodied the energy and force behind the machine. In contrast, the clerks (Jack's brother Dan Casement pushed paper with equal intensity) are seen in a more "civilized" setting, though the board-and-bat shanties look rough. The photographer has removed this group from the construction, both in environment and class. His composition is reminiscent of Paul Strand's classic portraits, which it predates. Even more remote are the dignitaries, shown by Russell in a strictly man-made environment. The lavishly appointed parlor car of the vice-president bears no relationship to the brute force that got it there.

As the steel rails raced to infinity, pushing the untouched land before them like glacial fingers, Russell and his photographic assistants logged the miles on their glass plates. The captain chronicled as much as his camera could encompass. When he saw a strong picture possibility he took several shots, each with a slightly different viewpoint. His experience guided him well, for though he had a well-practiced intuitive sense he did not trust it entirely. He left the decision on the best viewpoint for a later time; the particular moments of the history-making event would not be repeated. At some time or other in the trek, the photographer's camera focused on every aspect of the megamachine—on the people to whom the power had been delegated and the forces behind it. He caught the will of a nation in progress—nothing in nature withstood the momentum. If the natural order of things defied the parallel track, steam-driven machinery and dynamite removed the impediment.

Unlike the year before, construction continued through the winter of 1868. A virtual army of workers now filled the landscape, tunneling in or cutting through

it. The land gave way to the economy of the flat bed. By the end of 1868 the crew had logged more than four hundred miles of track and the Union Pacific had reached the Utah border.

The Union Pacific and the Central Pacific raced on at a furious pace. For each mile of steel ribbon measured out, enormous monetary gain was realized, and the competitors would have been happy to track right past each other in the rush for profit. Fortunately, Congress finally decreed in April that the meeting point would be Promontory Summit. To reach the designated point the Union Pacific crew—in thirty-eight days and nights —engineered and built a trestle up the east face of the promontory that spanned 400 feet and stood 85 feet high. East and West would be united at Promontory Point, the marriage date set for 10 May 1869.

A town materialized for the ceremony and the day arrived. Three photographers stood in readiness to record the union. There was the usual flurry of last-minute problems (officials disagreed on which railroad had the honor of driving the last spike), but finally the dignitaries assembled and everyone eagerly awaited the event. Alfred Hart, official photographer for the Central Pacific; Charles Savage, the Mormon photographer of Salt Lake City; and Andrew J. Russell stood ready. Officialdom gathered in front of the straight-stacked engine and removed its collective hat for the photographers.

The ceremony began. Russell and the other photographers preserved the scene in several poignant and timely photographs. It was Russell's photograph of this moment that became the pictorial basis for Thomas Hill's painting *Driving of the Last Spike*. The Union Pacific photographer, however, caught the essence of the event in a single image. In that view the railway, the telegraph (heightened by a solitary figure standing atop the pole), and a camera in the foreground stand in readiness to signal a new age. The *Philadelphia Photographer* had editorialized two years earlier: "Nothing seems beyond the reach of photography. It is the railway and the telegraph of art. The telegraph detects and catches the thief, and so does photography. The railways carry us to points afar, and so does photography—it does more."[6] The words seem prophetic, for those three elements—the railway, the telegraph, and "the railway and the telegraph of art"—pictured together in a remote, dusty plain would alter forever America's vision of itself.

At last the spike was driven and the message signaled to the world in that blow: "Done!" With pomp and pronouncements over, the real celebration began. The two engines moved forward, and Captain Russell captured the most famous moment of the entire happening—the chief engineers of the two railways shaking hands as bottles of champagne bridged the chasm that had once been two thousand miles long.

With the frantic race over, Russell and his photographic team turned a more leisurely eye on the land surrounding the railroad. They photographed the populated West—the towns and settlements as well as the settlers themselves—and made promotional views for the railroad. The eastern-bred photographer now found the time to correspond not only with his hometown paper but with *Anthony's Photographic Bulletin*, revealing himself to be a perceptive and lively storyteller with a good sense of humor and a hearty fellow who took things in stride. He wrote amusing anecdotes and explained the ways of the West for his eastern readership.

The captain and his two companion-photographers traveled about for several months, following the Promontory link-up, making images. They returned to photograph some of the engineering feats and were able to document their construction in a calmer atmosphere. (Russell captured the dramatic testing of the Devil's Gate bridge with three locomotives atop.) They focused their lenses on new subject matter—the relationship of the man-made to the land—for the track threw everything else into a new perspective.

In short, Andrew Russell made a complete visual document of the railroad and its environs. He focused not only on the spectacular but also on the kitsch aspects of nature, obvious benchmarks such as "Thousand Mile Tree," and landmarks like Skull Rock which became familiar to tourists as scenic wonders.

In August, outside Bear River City, Russell's group encountered the King party and joined them as King rounded out his third year of the survey. They traveled together for several weeks on an unofficial basis and Russell made some fine images of the surveying party that were included in the body of the King survey photographs. They stand in distinct contrast to the work of O'Sullivan, whose attempts at portraiture were so often strained; as Russell's photographs show, the men clearly responded to his command.

Leaving the King party, Russell continued on to the

end of the track in Sacramento. That was Central Pacific territory which had been covered by A. A. Hart, so the Union Pacific crew made fewer images.

Captain Russell worked for the Union Pacific Railroad for more than two years, carrying out his commission. Once he returned to his home in New York he apparently never ventured West again, with or without a camera. Unlike William Henry Jackson, who had gone West in search of opportunity, Russell had been sought out by the railroad to enhance the corporate opportunity. He had been a model company man, and the Union Pacific had paid him well for his work. Perhaps for that reason he either was not interested in, or thought it improper to exploit his work personally. A single volume intended as the first in a series of portfolios was issued in 1869 by the Union Pacific (*The Great West Illustrated* . . .), but no further volumes materialized. A year later, Ferdinand Hayden used thirty Russell images, reduced in size to 6 by 8 inches, in his publication *Sun Pictures of Rocky Mountain Scenery*. The prints were neither as sharp nor as spectacular as Russell's larger versions since reduction was most likely done by means of the "solar camera" technique, which also reduced clarity. Hayden's book sold far more copies than the Union Pacific volume, however, because it was one-third the price, but it did not bring Russell the fame that other photographers managed to claim.

The captain turned over his negatives to a promoter named Stephen Sedgwick, originally one of his assistants, who had returned East to become a sales agent and lecturer. But with the advent of the dry plate and the end of Sedgwick's lectures, any profit that Russell may have made from his western negatives had been fully realized. During these years Russell maintained a studio in New York, but in 1891, although only sixty-one years of age, the photographer applied for a disability pension from the military. He died eleven years later.

Captain Andrew J. Russell operated largely independently, as he carried his camera into an unknown land among widely divergent people and conditions. He had little in the way of tradition or historical precedent to follow, but the body of work he produced for the Union Pacific is thoroughly consistent and competent. He possessed a well-developed sense of the elements of composition, no doubt a result of his experience as a painter and illustrator, and a feel for the significant picture. He also had an uncanny ability to depict scale. As few others could, he transmitted a true sense of the vastness of the West and the feeling of space that unfailingly impressed those who traversed that land.

Russell was one of the earliest to capture the essence of the megamachine—the organization and American will behind it—that would later rocket men to the moon. He created a visual document that merits careful study and a bow of admiration.

NOTES

1. In correspondence he referred to Lewis M. Rutherford's photographs of the moon, and he may have been a fellow member of the Photographical Society of New York. See Andrew J. Russell, "On

the Mountains with the Tripod and Camera," *Anthony's Photographic Bulletin* 1 (1870): 35.

2. Andrew J. Russell, *The Great West Illustrated in a Series of Photographic Views Across the Continent: Taken Along the Line of the Union Pacific Railroad, West from Omaha, Nebraska*, vol. 1 (New York, 1869), p. ii.

3. Andrew J. Russell, "A New Out-Door Camera Box," *Anthony's Photographic Bulletin* 1 (1870): 117–18.

4. Barry B. Combs, *Westward to Promontory* (Palo Alto, Calif.: American West Publishing Co., 1969), p. 43.

5. Ibid., p. 50.

6. "Photosculpture," *Philadelphia Photographer* 4 (1867): 105.

70.   PROMONTORY TRESTLE, ENGINE NO. 119

71.   TUNNEL NO. 3, WEBER CANYON

72.   GENERAL JOHN S. CASEMENT AND HIS OUTFIT. 1867–68

73. PROMONTORY POINT, MAY 10, 1869

74. PROMONTORY POINT: THE CEREMONY STARTS, MAY 10, 1869

75.   MORMON SURVEYORS. 1869

76. LOG CABIN OF SAMUEL AND MARY BUNTING ASTON, WITH GATHERING
OF RELATIVES, SALT LAKE

77. ECHO CITY AT THE HEAD OF WEBER CANYON, A MORMON FARMING
COMMUNITY. 1868

78. SKULL ROCK, DALE CREEK CANYON, WYOMING TERRITORY. 1867–68

79.   DAN CASEMENT AND CLERKS AT ECHO CITY, DAN STANDING IN DOORWAY. 1867–68

80. HYDRAULIC GOLD MINING NEAR DUTCH FLATS, CALIFORNIA

81. "SPHYNX OF THE VALLEY"

82.   ON THE MOUNTAINS OF GREEN RIVER. 1867–68

FOLLOWING THE TRACKS:
ARUNDEL C. HULL (1846–1908)

By the spring of 1867, the Union Pacific's sprint westward had become a marathon, leaving swirls and eddies in its wake that sometimes settled into a town, more often back into dust.

Arundel C. Hull, a young photographer who lived in Omaha where the great race began, outfitted a photographic rig and climbed aboard a westbound train. He had decided to follow the tracks as far as they could take him and to travel on his own, by any conveyance, wherever they could not. He preceded Captain Andrew J. Russell, making one of the earliest documents of a land laid bare by the incision of the iron rails.[1]

Hull traveled throughout Colorado, Wyoming, and Utah for a year and a half, selling views to sustain his wanderings. He arrived in some locations almost at the moment of their creation, and his lens captured the rawness of the life and people who stayed to forge a town as the iron horse moved on. In October, 1868, he photographed Laramie, Wyoming, in its infant stage—barely five months old.

He made views of one western town after another—the elements that composed them, the people who lived in them, the landscape that surrounded them—and he did so competently. One town seems indistinguishable from another, and a pattern begins to emerge in his work that transcends time and locale, for Arundel Hull's camera was in fact documenting the taming and civilizing

experience in its initial stages. Everywhere he photographed, the roughness of this newly created West comes through—in the shelters, in the eyes of the people, and in the images of men hanged from a tree. The law was what men decided it was at the moment and, on that subject, Hull was very much a man of the West. When he was setting up his camera to record the hanging of Sam Dugan, he was outraged to see another would-be reporter doing the same. The *Rocky Mountain News* reported, "We are told certain artists were fighting over it this morning for the exclusive privilege of taking photographic views of it,"[2] but apparently both walked away with images.

When he returned to Omaha he found employment with the Jackson Brothers, and the following year, 1869, found him in the company of William Henry, revisiting familiar territory. Jackson described Hull as "an experienced camera man and a willing worker,"[3] and the pair traveled for several months, making salable views, retracing many of Hull's earlier steps in their westward photographic venture. "Hull has done all the running about, as I prefer doing the darkroom work of coating and developing plates,"[4] wrote Jackson, and obviously he relied on the experienced eye of the veteran field photographer to choose and compose many of the views. The team traveled throughout the summer on the just-completed transcontinental railroad and returned with the

83.   JACK MORROW AT BENTON, WYOMING TERRITORY. 1868

season's experience on hundreds of pieces of glass. "With these views," Jackson wrote, "I was sure I could establish myself as a front-rank scenic photographer,"[5] which is precisely what he did. It will probably never be known which of those views were, in fact, made by Arundel Hull. Like many an early photographer employed by a gallery, Hull was not credited—unfortunately, a common practice.[6] It is certain that these views, seen by Ferdinand Hayden in 1870, prompted Hayden to choose Jackson to accompany his survey. Hull could as easily have been the choice, but few knew what he, perhaps, never forgot—that he might have been where William Henry Jackson was had his name been on those photographs. He left the employ of Jackson Brothers and settled into a gallery of his own in a small town.

Independently, Arundel Hull had undertaken an incredibly ambitious documentation of the early West and had made some extraordinary images. He claimed to have made a photograph of Sitting Bull on that solo western journey. Unfortunately, many of his views made on that first trip, prepared as he went along and often in primitive conditions, were not signed. Traveling as he did for more than a year and a half, he could not keep all of his latent images and reused his glass. His work was even known to the artist Thomas Moran, who spent several days as a guest in the Hulls' home and selected views from which to work. But the vagaries of fate relegated the work of this early photographer to obscurity.

In the 1920s, unknown to Hull's family, a photographer who had leased his studio hauled a life's work to the city dump. Thus has much of the imagery of the early West met its end.

NOTES

1. Biographical information on A. C. Hull is taken from Nina Hull Miller, *Shutters West* (Denver: Sage Books, 1962).

2. Ralph W. Andrews, *Picture Gallery Pioneers* (Seattle: Superior Pub. Co., 1964), p. 147.

3. William H. Jackson, *Time Exposure* (New York: G. P. Putnam's Sons, 1940), p. 176.

4. Ibid., p. 180.

5. Ibid., p. 176.

6. Mathew Brady claimed credit for all the Civil War photographs done under his aegis, undoubtedly a bitter experience for many photographers. It became well known that Alexander Gardner left Brady's gallery for that reason, and went on to establish his own gallery.

84. DANCE HOUSE AT LARAMIE. 1868

85. FREUND'S GUN STORE AT LARAMIE, WYOMING TERRITORY.
1868

86.   STEVE YOUNG HANGED AT LARAMIE BY VIGILANTES. OCTOBER 19, 1868

87. OUTLAWS HANGED AT LARAMIE BY VIGILANTES. BIG NED, CON WAGNER, AND ACE MOORE. OCTOBER 18, 1868

88. SAM DUGAN HANGED BY VIGILANTES AT DENVER. DECEMBER 1, 1868

THE BUFFALO HUNT:
GEORGE ROBERTSON
(active c. 1868 – 74)

To many a white man the buffalo was simply a curiosity. Dr. William A. Bell, the English physician-turned-photographer, described them as "curious freaks of nature. . . . The small hind quarters look out of all proportion to the massive strength of the shoulders and chest; smooth, and apparently shaven, like the back of a French poodle, they do not seem to belong to the same animal."[1] His description no doubt evoked a mixture of wonder and amusement. To the Indian, however, the buffalo was a way of life and a means of independence. As he witnessed the unbelievable near-extinction of the vast herds of shaggy beasts, he perceived within it his own destruction.

The railroad brought not only hide-hunters anxious to supply eastern markets with robes and tongues (considered a delicacy), but also the thrill seeker and casual traveler who shot at animals from railroad cars for diversion.

Buffalo hunting became a lucrative enterprise, and one curious photographer decided to join a Texas hunting party to record the event as part of a series illustrating life on the frontier. The photographer was George Robertson, who had worked in the Washington, D.C., gallery of Alexander Gardner and had been lured from his cosmopolitan employment by an Austin, Texas, studio in 1872.[2] He arrived at a time when Texas west of the Hundredth Meridian was still in a "pioneer condition" and life on that frontier decidedly lively, but apparently it suited his photographic taste.

Described as "mechanical, something of a tinkerer by disposition," he seems to have been one of the few to venture into the frontier areas of the state. Unfortunately, scarcely any of the many images Robertson made have survived.[3]

Pictures of live herds obviously eluded his slow wet plates, but he recorded events of the hunt once the huge beasts had been felled—the skinning, salting, and drying of meat and skins. What his plates could not document was the reckless devastation and wanton waste left behind once the hunters had their hides. "From the bulls we often took nothing but the tongue," particularly if the hide was "thick and scabby," one seasoned hunter later noted. Nor could Robertson's plates record the meaning of the near-total decimation of the buffalo, which brought an end to the Plains Indians' freedom more swiftly and surely than any army. In 1876 a newspaper reported that in a single day one hundred wagons carrying ninety to one hundred hides each could be counted on the road from Dallas to Weatherford, Texas.[4] The account documented a common occurrence throughout the entire stretch of the Great Plains. In 1880 buffalo had far outnumbered cattle in Montana, but within three

89.   SKINNING A BUFFALO ON THE PRAIRIE. "MEAT FOR DINNER." 1874

years they had all but disappeared. "I came upon this road, following the buffalo that my wives and children might have their cheeks plump and their bodies warm. Do not ask us to give up the buffalo for the sheep," the Indian had pleaded.[5] But his voice had been drowned in the thunder of the wholesale slaughter.

Within a few decades the hunters had turned a sea of buffalo into a trail of bleached bones. Robertson, too, seems to have disappeared, leaving behind almost as little trace.

NOTES

1. William A. Bell, *New Tracks in North America*, 2 vols. (London: Chapman & Hall, 1869–70), 1: 38.

2. Walter Prescott Webb, "A Texas Buffalo Hunt with Original Photographs," *Holland's Magazine* (1927): 10–11; 101–2. Unless otherwise stated, quotes in this chapter are taken from this source.

3. Curiously, very little visual documentation of the settling years in Texas has been uncovered. McArthur Cullen Ragsdale, a West Texas photographer, traveled over the state from 1875 until he opened a permanent studio in San Angelo in 1881, but most of his early work is lost. A collection of later work does exist at the Fort Concho Museum, Fort Concho, Texas.

4. *Galveston News* (Texas), 6 June 1876.

5. Speech of Ten Bears before the Treaty Council at Medicine Lodge, as quoted in Dee Brown, *Bury My Heart at Wounded Knee* (New York: Holt, Rinehart & Winston, 1970), pp. 241–42.

90.   CAMP OF BUFFALO HUNTERS ON EVANS CREEK. SCAFFOLDS FOR DRYING BUFFALO MEAT. 1874

91. THE BUFFALO HUNT. A PRAIRIE CAMP. 1874

92. AT EASE IN THE BUFFALO CAMP. 1874

THE INDIAN: WILL SOULE
(1836 – 1908)

William S. Soule's arrival in the West coincided with the Indian's attempt to reconcile himself to semi-reservation life. The photographer had suffered a severe wound in the Civil War, and in 1867, still not fully recovered and with his studio in Chambersburg, Pennsylvania, standing in charred ruins, he felt in need of change.[1]

With new photographic equipment in tow he headed for Saint Louis, and when a job as clerk in the camp store at Fort Dodge became available, he took it. He began to photograph in his free time, and it was the Indian that seemed to claim his attention. Many of the principals who had signed the Medicine Lodge Treaty, as well as numerous members of the tribes who would try to live by it, passed before his lens.

Soule accepted the position of post photographer at Fort Sill in 1869, but on his own time he continued to record the Indian faces that would become more elusive within a few years. His private photographic pursuits proved as lucrative as his official position, for he sent the negatives to his brother in the East, where the images were a highly popular commercial item. John Soule produced not only individual prints but albums as well, and copyrighted much of his brother's work in 1873.

From a photographic standpoint, William Soule's Indian portraits are rather ordinary, but they are extraordinary—and were so even in their own day—for the costumes and trappings in which the Indians chose to be photographed. The Kiowa Chief Stumbling Bear is wearing Major General Winfield Scott Hancock's full-dress coat and shoulder straps, "loaned him for the occasion by the general."[2] Two photographs of Comanche chiefs show Asatoyeh wearing an enlisted man's jacket and carrying a revolver, while Tosawi sports a "Jeff Davis" military hat. In Soule's image of three Wichita squaws, the fact that the Indian women appear bare-breasted was in keeping with what was a natural and customary practice, and therefore they undoubtedly posed willingly.

Soule stayed in the West for only seven years. During that time of troubling change his camera documented a people who had surrendered their arms but not their wills: the braves faced his lens squarely and held themselves proudly. When he left the West in 1874 he took with him many an Indian who would never again be captured—either on glass or in spirit.

NOTES

1. Having worked in his older brother John's Boston-based studio, Soule gave his occupation as photographer upon enlistment in the army, but it is not known whether he had the opportunity or desire to photograph the Civil War. See Wilbur Sturtevant Nye, *Plains Indian Raiders* (Norman: University of Oklahoma Press, 1968), p. ix.

93. SA-LO-SO (TSA'L-AU-TE, CRY OF THE WILD GOOSE), SON OF SANTANTA.
KIOWA TRIBE. C. 1867–74

2. Notes made by Brig. Gen. Philip Reade on photographic prints of William S. Soule in Album 189, Huntington Library, San Marino, California. Reade spent some time in a Kiowa village in the fall of 1868, as noted on one photograph, and seems to have been acquainted with Soule.

94.   THREE WICHITA SQUAWS. 1868

95. SET-TAIN-TE OR WHITE BEAR, CALLED SATANTA. BORN C. 1830;
DIED 1878, BY SUICIDE. KIOWA TRIBE. C. 1870

96. TOSH-A-WAY (TOSAWI), A COMANCHE CHIEF. 1868

97.   STUMBLING BEAR, A KIOWA CHIEF [PHOTO TAKEN IN 1867 NEAR FORT DODGE, KANSAS]

98.   ASA-TON-YEH (ASATOYEH), A COMANCHE CHIEF. 1868

THE FRONTIER YEARS: LATON ALTON HUFFMAN (1854–1931)

A few years and many miles removed from Soule's outpost, the same principals—the military and the Indian—came before the lens of another young photographer, Laton Alton Huffman.[1]

Having learned photography in the collodion era, working for F. J. Haynes, he arrived in 1878 at Fort Keogh, Montana Territory, to assume the position of post photographer, as Will Soule had done at Fort Sill a decade earlier. It was less than two years after the Battle of the Little Big Horn and less than one year since Chief Joseph's surrender and his unforgettable pronouncement: "I am tired; my heart is sick and sad. From where the sun now stands I will fight no more forever." Both the Sioux and Cheyenne had surrendered at Fort Keogh, and when the twenty-four-year-old photographer arrived, the Indians, "prisoners of war," lived in their own camps near the fort, not yet forced to move to reservations. His studio became a gathering place at the fort for soldier and Indian alike. Huffman photographed them all—the noble visages of the chiefs who had brought about Custer's destruction as well as the army that in turn dealt the same fate to the pyrrhic victors.

In 1880 Huffman opened a studio in Miles City, which had become the locus of the cattle empire. The town and Huffman's studio saw many colorful people, both famous and infamous, pass through—Calamity Jane, Theodore Roosevelt, even members of the nobility. Regrettably, the photographer did much of his studio portrait work with the wet-plate collodion process, largely as an economy measure, and in reusing the glass he wiped some historic faces from his plates. Like Soule, however, he found that the portraits of Indians were among his best-selling commercial offerings, and these images brought him a brisk business.

It was a decade of movement in Montana Territory, where every aspect of the taming of the West could be found. Unlike the early exploration photographers who, by and large, were unconcerned with posterity, Laton Alton Huffman was aware of the significance of his times and prepared to make his own last stand photographically before the disappearing frontier. He trekked all over Montana Territory in the 1880s, documenting the days before barbed wire.[2] He traveled and explored with Yellowstone Kelly; he made scenic views of Yellowstone (some of which Ferdinand Hayden purchased); he acted as guide for game hunters and photographed both the wildlife and the hunt. He photographed the open range, using dry plates as soon as they became available to capture its rapidly changing countenance. He wrote: "I am making all my outside work instantaneous now sun or no sun and with wide open lens. . . . I shall soon show you what can be done from the saddle without ground glass or tripod . . . many of the best exposed when my horse was in motion."[3] Huffman's lens witnessed the

99.   JERK-LINE 12 ON THE OLD NORTH MONTANA FREIGHT ROAD

domination of the range pass from the great buffalo to herds of cattle and sheep, and finally to the barbed wire that reduced the vast space to human measure.

He perceived the multiple phases and the impact of the disappearing West: "Round about us the army of buffalo hunters—red men and white—were waging the final war of extermination upon the last great herds of American bison seen upon this continent. Then came the cattleman, the 'trail boss' with his army of cowboys, and the great cattle roundups. Then the army of railroad builders. That—the railway—was the fatal coming. One looked about and said, 'This is the last West.' It was not so. There *was* no more West after that. It was a dream and a forgetting, a chapter forever closed."[4] With the closing of that chapter, Huffman's spirited photographic ventures also ended.

In the 1890s the restless photographer moved about, tried various other cities, and even served in the Montana House of Representatives in 1893. He was searching for a place where the "West" still existed, but returned to Miles City near the end of the decade.

In 1905 he realized that the West did in fact exist and was very much in demand—in his photographs. Like William Henry Jackson, he found a new market for his old negatives and began to reproduce his early work in a variety of formats: postcards, enlargements up to seven feet long, contact prints, and hand-tinted enlargements and gravure plates. His copyrighted western views provided him with a living throughout his lifetime (he died in 1931), and they continue to be printed and sold today.

L. A. Huffman was not a photojournalist who simply dropped in on the scene to take from it what was newsworthy. From his earliest days at Fort Keogh, he carried a sense of the historic importance of the events and people about him: "In my studio [Captain William Philo] Clark and Little Wolf in those days conspired together to not only translate the sign language, but to photograph the living Indian in the various attitudes. But that, with many another dream of Clark's and mine . . . is passed away. The Indians didn't take kindly to it, and we couldn't make it go."[5] Even as he wrote those words, photographer Edward Curtis had joined the Harriman Expedition in the company of George Bird Grinnell, who began to plant the seeds of a similar yet far more ambitious idea.

Huffman carried a notebook along with his camera, making notes and diary entries on many of his photographic subjects and collecting background material, with the eventual intention of writing a book. The book was never written, but his images of the frontier years, some of which "cost more than a week of riding, watching and waiting"[6] on the open range, are powerful documents of a past age. They are visual recollections of the first order.

NOTES

1. Much of the information in this chapter can be found in the two-volume biography by Mark H. Brown and W. R. Felton: *The Frontier Years: L. A. Huffman, Photographer of the Plains* (New York: Bramhall House, 1955), and *Before Barbed Wire: L. A. Huffman,*

Photographer on Horseback (New York: Henry Holt and Co., 1956).

2. Huffman wrote, "I would that there were yet a few waste places left untouched by the settler and his cursed wire fence, good in its way, but not for me. I can not help it." Brown and Felton, *The Frontier Years*, p. 52.

3. Ibid., p. 43.

4. Ibid., p. 26.

5. Ibid., p. 41.

6. Brown and Felton, *Before Barbed Wire*, p. 37.

100. HARVEY TRUSLER'S RANCH

Going to the Roundup. 1890

101.   GOING TO THE ROUNDUP. C. 1890

102.   THE HONYOCKER

103.   OLD TIME CHUCK WAGON. 1885

N Bar Crossing, Powder River 1886

104.   N BAR CROSSING, POWDER RIVER. 1886

105. BUFFALO SKINNERS—"TAKING THE MONSTER'S ROBE," NORTHERN MON-
TANA. JANUARY, 1882

106. BULL TRAIN AT MAIN AND PARK STREETS, MILES CITY, MONTANA TERRI-
TORY. 1881

107.   A SIOUX WARRIOR'S GRAVE. 1879

SETTLERS AND SODDIES: SOLOMON D. BUTCHER (1856–1927)

From the wilds of Montana Territory to the Great Plains, the shape and content of the land were rapidly changing. While some, such as L. A. Huffman, felt constrained by barbed wire, others recognized that their horizons and opportunities would grow as the land yielded to settlement.

In Custer County, Nebraska, a photographer named Solomon D. Butcher perceived that he belonged to a passing way of life. The year 1882 found him farming, though he disliked it, and making photographs, when he could, in his photographic studio of sod. "Whenever anyone wanted a tintype I dropped my hoe and made it and went back to the field again."[1]

Perhaps as an escape from the monotony and drudgery of breaking the soil Solomon Butcher launched on a self-appointed task with near-missionary zeal: to record the settlers and the events, and the way of life of the land of which he was a part. "From the time I thought of the History Book, for seven days and nights it drove sleep from my eyes. I laid out plans and covered sheet after sheet of paper, only to tear them up and consign them to the wastebasket. At last, Eureka! Eureka! I had found it! I was so elated that I had lost all desire for rest. . . . I told my scheme to every one I met. I talked about it constantly."[2]

In the summer of 1886 he embarked upon his mission

as conscious historian of the settling experience as he saw it and lived it in Custer County, Nebraska. He traveled about in a wagon photographing the churches, schools, prize bulls, fairs—anything, however minute or seemingly insignificant, that comprised a piece of the historical puzzle. Once he began, he pursued his project with tireless resolve, his zeal carrying him through the drudgery of farming that supported him and his family. He worked for years gathering not only photographs but written histories of the people and of the events they recounted to him. He even went so far as to re-create photographically some of the noteworthy moments that had textured the history of Custer County, using the same participants when possible. These photographs appear painfully contrived and out of keeping with the carefully documented main body of his work, which eventually numbered thousands of pictures.

Butcher made hundreds of photographs that are variations on a single theme—a family posed in front of its sod house. The elements and rhythms are repeated in image after image, yet from the monotony and sameness of these pictures—because Butcher sought the whole rather than the representative part—evolves a document of the pattern of settling as it recurred throughout the West. Every photograph shows evidence of the inventive adaptation that created a life in a new land as similar as

108.   W. H. BLAIR OF HUCKLEBERRY, NEAR BROKEN BOW, NEBRASKA. 1888

possible to the one left behind. Settlers seemed to have gone West only to reconstitute the society they had established on countless eastern frontiers.

With the sun at his back, Butcher composed the actuality of a settler's spread, his camera unerringly including the elements that prairie life dictated. The sod house, a structure born of necessity and the lack of other material, sheltered most of the population. A special tool known as a "grasshopper plow" had been devised to cut a uniformly thick slice of sod into long strips. From these, bricks could be cut of uniform size, an acre of land usually providing enough sod to build a house. With this tool, the prairie had been transformed into homes that varied only slightly from spread to spread. Livestock figured in nearly every picture, a horse and cow the lifeblood of existence. The family itself was assembled, all present and accounted for if possible, for Butcher wanted a record of every member of the community.

Within the same photograph, the settler composed the life he had imported. He moved his furniture into the yard in front of his house; he dressed himself and his children in clothes obviously not suited to his prairie existence but rather for his "civilized" image; he proudly displayed the accouterments of civilization if he possessed them. Sewing machines appear, and in one extraordinary photograph an organ stands boldly at the center of the picture. One can guess at the effort and desire it represents.

Butcher's photographic style and imagery evolved out of the historical task he had assigned himself. He obviously did not reap much financial success from his ven-

tures. Even when families paid for prints to send back East to relatives, payment often consisted of a few chickens or a good meal and bed for the night. "The country was new and the people not overburdened with money," and he probably felt obliged to provide a print or two for a family who had obviously made an effort to gather everything before his lens.[3]

In seven years the peripatetic Butcher made more than 1,500 glass records and filled a hundred notebooks with histories, but the immediate demands of his own existence on the prairie forced him to postpone taking his ambitious scheme any further. Then, in 1899, his house went up in flames. He lost most of the prints and nearly all the written histories, but the negatives were spared.

He started again, and, fifteen years after he had begun his project, Butcher's *Pioneer History of Custer County* was published in an edition of 1,000 copies, for which he himself raised much of the money. It was an expensive book to produce, containing 400 pages and 200 photographic reproductions, and was the only collection of his work that was printed in his lifetime. (Curiously, only about twenty of the photographs in the book are of "soddies." Perhaps it all seemed commonplace and trivial to Butcher by the time he finally brought his work to fruition.)

In recent years the *Pioneer History* has been reprinted and the collection itself has become the subject of repeated study—for its specific details of people of different nationalities, of landscape and terrain, and tools; for its evocation of the pioneer experience; and for the larger meanings contained in the record of how society constitutes and reconstitutes itself. But Solomon Butcher died with the belief that his idea had ended a dismal failure.

NOTES

1. John I. White, "Pages from a Nebraska Album," *The American West* 12 (1975): 30.

2. Harry E. Chrisman, "The Sod House Photographs," *The West* 9 (1968): 31.

3. White, *op. cit.*, p. 31.

109. JAKE PLUM, ROSE VALLEY, 8 OR 9 MILES NORTHEAST OF BROKEN BOW, NEBRASKA, EAST CUSTER COUNTY. C. 1887–88

110. HARVEY ANDREWS FAMILY AT GRAVE ON THEIR OWN FARM NEAR NEW HELENA AND VICTORIA CREEK IN CEDAR CANYON. LEFT TO RIGHT: MARY ANDREWS, CHARLES HENRY ANDREWS, HARVEY B. ANDREWS, MRS. JENNIE ANDREWS HOLDING DAUGHTER LILLIAN

III. FONT SHARP CATTLE RANCH, 1889, EAST OF ANSLEY, NEBRASKA, SHOWING HIS THOROUGHBRED TROTTERS

112.   THE ADVOCATE OFFICE AT ANSLEY, NEBRASKA. 1889

113.   COLONEL KILLGORE, RIVERDALE, BUFFALO COUNTY. 1903

114.   SNAKE RIVER FALLS, CHERRY COUNTY, SOUTHWEST OF VALENTINE,
       NEBRASKA

115.   CUSTER COUNTY. 1888. "WE DID NOT WANT TO SHOW THE OLD SOD HOUSE TO FRIENDS BACK EAST, BUT THE YOUNG LADY AND MOTHER WANTED TO PROVE THEY OWNED AN ORGAN."

116.   JAMES PIERCE, OLD SUMMERFORD P. O. ON SAND CREEK, CUSTER COUNTY. 1886

THE MORMON SETTLERS:
GEORGE EDWARD ANDERSON
(1860 – 1928)

A thousand miles away from Solomon Butcher another photographer shared a similar sense of history and purpose. But George Edward Anderson, the son of Mormon converts from England and Scotland, was further motivated by a religious commitment to his community. Beginning early, under the tutelage of the well-known photographer C. R. Savage, he found his true calling, and remains one of the best photographers yet to emerge from the dry-plate era.[1]

His years in the Savage studio were brief but formative. He acquired expertise with the photographic process and came to know the people Savage's gallery attracted, among them the painter John Hafen, who became a lifelong friend. At the age of seventeen George Edward felt ready—or perhaps compelled—to become independent. He opened a studio in Salt Lake but stayed only a few years. In the early 1880s, he moved to Springville, Utah, and bought a house that Hafen baptized the "artist's retreat."

For most of the next two decades Ed, as he was called, photographed the people of the communities scattered throughout central Utah, while a partner named L. D. Crandall conducted much of the regular studio work. Anderson traveled with the standard portable tent and painted backdrops, but he was not an ordinary photogra-

pher by any measure. His photographic eye became increasingly inventive and refined, and he began to arrange his subjects in outdoor settings in poses that were neither contrived nor stiff. Working in natural light, he learned to compose groups of all sizes extremely well. Anderson was more than an itinerant camera operator, for he belonged to the community of believers—and thus he did not merely pass through a place but became, in spirit, part of it. As a Mormon he understood the inward and outward struggles of the Mormon settlers who had come to that land to worship and to make the earth fruitful. He was sensitive to their aspirations and achievements, however meager these may have seemed in what was then so poor an area.

Anderson photographed many of his subjects going about their labors. His people seem to have been arrested in the midst of their work, their tools and goods about them, or else they seem to have been interrupted momentarily in the performance of a daily task. There is a sense of activity, and therefore vitality, in these pictures that few other photographers achieved. Particularly evocative are his images of people engaged in private activities. A young mother has dressed herself and her child fancifully and waits for the photographer a moment, poised beside her bicycle in a wood; a group of picnickers

117.   TENT HOME OF LACE MINER AND HIS FAMILY AMONG THE ASPENS

has allowed momentary intrusion on their party.

Anderson's camera—and spirit—found constant nourishment in his church and his work. He photographed the building of Mormon temples throughout central Utah, the church leaders, the pageants and gatherings the community shared.

Anderson experienced some financially lean years, particularly once he had a family, but he could not think in terms of remuneration—he simply wanted to make negatives day after day. Money to him was a necessary evil, but unfortunately there was not always enough of that evil in his life. He built a two-story studio, "G. E. Anderson Art Bazaar," which brought him financial chaos and a debt which took years to pay off, but he eventually worked his way clear.

In 1900 news of a mine tragedy near Scofield, Utah, reached him, and he rushed to record the event. It turned out to be the worst mine disaster to date in America, killing 199 men and boys and leaving the town with more than a hundred widows and more than 250 orphans. Anderson documented the events that followed and the human wreckage that resulted from the terrible explosion: rows of blackened bodies awaiting the last rites; the arrival of coffins; the simple pine boxes lying in flower-draped silence in a schoolroom, for want of any other space; the mass burial on a gravel-strewn hillside. Anderson's perceptive record of the tragedy is a first-rate work of photojournalism and reveals another aspect of his photographic talent. The photographs were, however, credited to Bedlington Lewis, a local Scofield photographer, both at the time of the disaster and later, but

they were subsequently authenticated as Anderson's work.

In 1907 the Church called upon him to undertake a mission to last some two to three years. The photographer, aged forty-seven, welcomed the appointment as an opportunity to fulfill his own mission as well—to make a complete photographic record of the history of the Mormon religion.

He departed in April, presumably for England, the designated destination, but the following year found the enigmatic photographer still in the United States pursuing his own quest—traveling to the places sacred to the Mormon movement and retracing the steps of Joseph Smith, the Mormon prophet.[2] He finally embarked for England, returning to the United States only in 1910. The passion to research and photograph the history of Mormonism had become an obsession, and when he at last came back to Springville it was after an absence of nearly seven years.

Once in the United States again, Anderson continued to photograph Mormon history. He sacrificed everything to it—family relationships, three years of his life, and all his money, making pictures on his travels only to support his study. Estranged from his family, he lived alone much of the time in the studio, but did not lose his passion to photograph. He sometimes borrowed photographic plates from other photographers, and once he reportedly borrowed a neighbor's wagon in order to go to town—and disappeared for three months.

Incredibly prolific, Anderson left tens of thousands of negatives when he died. It is an extraordinary body of work, a document of one of the significant religious forces in America as well as a sensitive portrayal of the people committed to it.

NOTES

1. Biographical information is taken from Nelson B. Wadsworth, *Through Camera Eyes* (Provo, Utah: Brigham Young University Press, 1975), pp. 159–70); and Rell G. Francis, "G. E. Anderson," *Popular Photography* 77 (1975): 86–97; 113–15.

2. The resulting photographs were published in John Henry Evans, *The Birth of Mormonism in Picture* (Salt Lake City: Deseret Sunday School Union, 1909).

118.   SCOFIELD SMITH SHOP, SCOFIELD, UTAH

119.   SILVER CITY BLACKSMITH SHOP, SILVER CITY, UTAH. C. 1890–1900

120. ETHER BLANCHARD FARM, MAPLETON, UTAH. 1902

121. STANLEY GARDNER SECTION CREW, INDIANOLA, UTAH. 1900

122.   JEX & SONS BROOM FACTORY, SPANISH FORK, UTAH. 1896

123.   WHEELER & CHILDS, UNDERTAKERS AND MARBLE WORKERS, SPRINGVILLE, UTAH. 1888

124. PROVO BOAT CLUB, FIRST LIGHTWEIGHT CREW. 1890

125. PART OF MINE RESCUE CREW AT THE SCOFIELD MINE DISASTER, MAY 1, 1900. WINTER QUARTERS, NO. 4 MINE

126. STRAWBERRY CANAL UNDER CONSTRUCTION, SALEM, UTAH. 1915

127.   ANDERSON'S EARLY SPRINGVILLE STUDIO. C. 1895

128.   INTERIOR OF ANDERSON'S STUDIO. C. 1914

129.   ANNA THOMPSON AND SOLDIERS, SPRINGVILLE, UTAH. 1898–99

130.   THE SAM BRAMALL FAMILY

131. MRS. DAVID FELT AND DAUGHTER, SPRINGVILLE, UTAH. 1898

THE COWBOY: ANDREW ALEXANDER FORBES (1862–1921)

One figure is present throughout collections of photographs from Montana to Texas and all points in between —the cowboy. Photographers neglected or ignored various aspects of the frontier, but cowboys, in every hole and corner, seem to have been found by camera men in the settling years even as today they continue to appear on the movie screen. "The stupendous Western Cowboy Legend can be subdivided into four major fantasies: the Myth of the Great Outdoors, with its reputation for cleansing and purifying the human spirit; the Fable of the Life of Perpetual Action and Adventure, with its tempering effect on masculine character; the Illusion of Existence as a Permanent Fancy-Dress Ball, with its constant inspiration to romantic individualism; and the Mirage of the Regal Splendor of the Courtly Ranch as a dazzling center for sustaining frontier chivalry."[1]

The folklore of the cowboy continues to claim the imagination of a worldwide following, but the abundant photographic evidence manifests a vastly different reality. No matter the territory, the same truths emerge about the life of a cowboy.

The cowboy legend spread as rapidly as the cattle empire. As soon as the railroad made western beef accessible to eastern tables, major arteries coursed through the plains running with streams of hooved food, and small towns along the tracks became brawling, booming cities. And as the herds of cattle expanded, so did the number of men whose lives revolved around them.

A young photographer in his thirties named Andrew Alexander Forbes was one of the many who chased the cattle and their keepers with his lens, traveling throughout Texas and Oklahoma on buckboard, horse, and even on muleback when bad roads made all else impossible. He journeyed from spread to spread with his dry plates and photographed the cowboy where—and as—he found him. He did not concern himself with the legend, but conducted a profitable business among the real cowpunchers as he roamed the cattle country in the late 1880s and 1890s.

The cowboys who met the photographer's eye—poised with their gear and paraphernalia—are unembellished, a horse and a hat the two indispensables that recur in image after image. In contrast to their later movie counterparts, the cowboys in Forbes's pictures wear casually fitting clothes of all sorts and descriptions. While some wear boots, many others have on ordinary shoes. A few tote guns, but the majority do not. They are rarely seen as tall and lean in the saddle, but rather as a motley assortment of men of all ages and descriptions. Their life was one of constant exposure to the elements—sun, dust, wind, rain—unrelieved and often extreme; dreary, monotonous days filled with the dogged routine of keeping the bawling beasts under control; aching isolation.

132. COWBOYS AROUND A CHUCKWAGON AT MEAL TIME

This was the reality, and it can be seen in those hardened, stoic faces that looked straightforwardly into the photographer's lens.

Forbes made a reasonable living from the cowhands, almost all of whom ordered a photograph or two to send to relatives or simply to adorn the bunkhouse, which was barren of nearly everything else. Many simply welcomed the photographer as a new face and consented to be photographed as a diversion from the daily grind. Andrew Forbes sold his prints for anything up to a dollar, depending on how many the subject ordered, and he stayed at a spread as long as he had orders.

Forbes's cowboy portraits provide a coherent social document of those who kept one of the significant forces in the settling of the West—the cattle empire—going. But cowboys were not the only subject that claimed the attention of this itinerant photographer. In his travels the young camera man photographed the emerging communities, and he witnessed one of the wildest and most chaotic manifestations of the settling of the West. In April, 1889, at noon on the appointed day, lands in the Cherokee Strip were to be opened for settlement. Thousands upon thousands of settlers gathered to claim unassigned lands, for claims had to be filed on the spot and no one was to be allowed onto the land until the cavalry gave the signal. Good land, which once had been all that the government possessed in abundance, had already become a scarce commodity; Oklahoma offered a last chance for many would-be homesteaders.

The numbers that waited to claim a place in the Oklahoma sun burgeoned into legions. The photographer intercepted the boomers waiting for the moment of the last land grab, and when the gun sounded he tried with his camera to capture the mad rush. Six hours later an "instant" town had sprung up, and one month later Forbes recorded Guthrie, a town of similar boom origins, with frame buildings standing erect. What he caught is a document of the settling experience, which had taken decades in other areas, capsulized into a matter of days.

In 1909 Forbes left his cowboys to their hard life in Oklahoma and Texas and moved to California, where he established a studio.[2]

If his life on the open range had been half so arduous as that of the cowboys he faithfully portrayed, one does not wonder at his decision.

NOTES

1. Owen Ulph, "No Trade for Heroes," *The American West* 5 (1968): 17.

2. Scant biographical information exists on A. A. Forbes. A brief genealogy of the Forbes family in the Western History Collections, University of Oklahoma Library, Norman, and the above-noted article by Ulph reveal something of the photographer's early career. From 1909 on he was a pioneer photographer in the area of Bishop, California.

133.   FOUR MEN CAMPED OUT AND WAITING FOR THE OPENING OF OKLAHOMA. 1889

134.   WALKER & M'COY SIGN COMPANY, NEXT TO CITY MARSHALL OFFICE ON HARRISON AVENUE, GUTHRIE, OKLAHOMA. 1889

135.   SOUTH SECOND STREET EJECTION OF SQUATTERS FROM CONTESTED TOWN SITE CLAIM. GUTHRIE, OKLAHOMA. MAY 23, 1889

136.   A VIEW OF DOWNTOWN OKLAHOMA CITY JUST WEST AND NORTH OF SANTA FE DEPOT, MADE SHORTLY AFTER
       THE OPENING RUN ON APRIL 22, 1889

137. GROUP OF HOME-SEEKERS IN CAMP ON THE LINE WAITING FOR THE RUN OF '89 WHICH OPENED THE UNASSIGNED
LANDS IN INDIAN TERRITORY. SIGN READS, "COFFEE HERE 10¢"

GERONIMO: CAMILLUS S. FLY
(1849-1901)

In the dry-plate era photographers, like settlers, experienced everything from near-starvation to success, and for both the outcome often depended on forces beyond their control. Nature and politics frequently determined the settler's fate. The photographer's prosperity was either inextricably linked to that of his community (unless he were possessed with a mission, like Anderson or Butcher) or to the photographic possibilities his sphere of operation offered for unique and highly salable views that attracted buyers elsewhere (like Huffman's Indian portraits and Yellowstone views). But a photographer, unlike many a settler, could pack his tools and move on to greener pastures.

It would seem curious that Camillus S. Fly left San Francisco in 1879 to settle in Tombstone, Arizona—except that, aside from being a photographer, he was described as "one of Tombstone's most persistent miners."[1] Why he stayed in that "helldorado of the cactus bottoms"[2] remains a quandary. As a miner he had no success; he tried his hand at being sheriff of Cochise County; later in his life, having separated from his wife, he tried to run photographic studios in Bisbee and Phoenix. He consistently failed at nearly every venture he undertook. Apparently his wife kept things going through the failures, for the newspaper commented that Mrs. Fly, "who is also an accomplished photographic artist will conduct the gallery in this city as usual."[3]

Fly tried to take advantage of every opportunity and to rise to an occasion when one presented itself, but Tombstone was not overabundantly endowed with subject matter, nor was the photographer always ready. The reputation of the town derived almost solely from the outlaws who at one time or other made their way to the "Town Too Tough to Die," and the lawmen who came in pursuit of them. Fly did make photographs of many of the notorious characters, including the principals of the OK Corral shootout, but they are notable largely because of the reputation of those he "caught" rather than for photographic ingenuity. One would have thought he had a highly salable item, but his portrayals even of the badmen are uninteresting, and for some reason he did not photograph the aftermath of the shootout even though it took place at 2:30 P.M. right outside his studio. One eyewitness stated that Bill Clanton fell and rose to fire again "when Mr. Fly took his revolver from him," so apparently he was there and in the thick of the action. Ike Clanton, one of the notorious brothers, escaped through the photographer's studio.

Camillus Fly did have one unique photographic opportunity, however, which arrived with General George Crook's column as it proceeded to Mexico to accept the surrender of Geronimo and his band of Apaches in March, 1886. Crook offered what was perhaps the last chance for anyone to capture "wild Indians,"

138.   LEFT TO RIGHT: GERONIMO AND NATCHES MOUNTED, NATCHES WITH HAT ON; SON OF GERONIMO STANDING
BY HIS SIDE (WHITE HORSE HOLDING NAHI'S BABY GIRL; GERONIMO; CHIEF NAICHE; AND FUN, CONSIDERED
THE BRAVEST FIGHTER OF GERONIMO'S BAND. 1886)

either photographically or bodily, for the wily Geronimo had remained an elusive subject, both from the military and the camera.

Fly joined Crook's group. A local account reported: "Mr. Fly, the photographer, saw his opportunity, and improved it fully: he took 'shots' at 'Geronimo' and the rest of the group, and with a 'nerve' that would have reflected undying glory on a Chicago drummer, coolly asked 'Geronimo' and the warriors with him to change positions, and turn their heads or faces, to improve the negative."[4] The *Los Angeles Times* correspondent Charles Lummis, who covered the event, described Fly as "a nervy photographer."[5]

Fly also took full financial advantage of the event. Four of his photographs were reproduced in *Harper's Weekly* in April and he copyrighted fifteen photographs of the Apache surrender in that same year. That series of images seems to have been the high point of his somewhat dubious career behind the camera, and after his death his wife published them in a book.[6]

Camillus Fly succumbed in—and perhaps to—Tombstone at age fifty-two. His death certificate reads, "Cause of death: acute alcoholism."

NOTES

1. *Tombstone Weekly Epitaph*, 16 January 1882.

2. Ralph W. Andrews, *Photographers of the Frontier West* (New York: Bonanza Books, 1965), p. 142.

3. *Tombstone Epitaph*, 17 December 1887.

4. John Gregory Bourke, *On the Border with Crook* (Chicago: Rio Grande Press, 1891), p. 476.

5. Charles F. Lummis, *General Crook and the Apache Wars*, ed. Turbese Lummis Fiske (Flagstaff, Ariz.: Northland Press, 1966), p. 25.

6. C. S. Fly, *Scenes in Geronimo's Camp; the Apache Outlaw and Murderer. . . .* (Tombstone, Ariz., 1905), privately published.

No. 176—Council between General Crook and Geronimo.

139. COUNCIL BETWEEN GENERAL CROOK AND GERONIMO. MARCH, 1886

140. GERONIMO AND THREE OF HIS WARRIORS IN THE SIERRA MADRES. MARCH, 1886

141.   BAND OF APACHES. 1886

THE LAST FRONTIER:
JOHN C. H. GRABILL
(active c. 1887–91)

Buffalo had all but disappeared and barbed wire measured off much of the West when the photographer John C. H. Grabill set foot in Sturgis, Dakota Territory, in October, 1886. Little is known about him, but he must already have been a competent photographer when he arrived, for the newspaper reported shortly thereafter that "J. C. H. Grabill, the photographer, has sent out about $150 worth of views to various parties in Wyoming since his arrival here."[1]

Grabill appears and disappears throughout the Dakota Territory in the late 1880s and early 1890s, leaving little trace of his personality except in the small number of photographs which have so far been unearthed. Yet he took his photography seriously, copyrighting much of his work and printing on the mount of his pictures the ominous warning: "A handsome reward given for detection of any one copying any of my photographic views." This warning appeared as early as 1891 on the photographs issued by the Grabill Portrait and View Company, Deadwood.

He covered a great deal of territory at the same time that L. A. Huffman was photographing the frontiers of Montana, not far away. Both made scenic views for commercial purposes. But unlike Huffman, Grabill focused his lens on the people and forces at work civilizing the land. He photographed miners at work using hydraulic mining methods that devastated the earth but capitalized the country. He composed a group of dapper engineers surveying for railway lines. Their clothes suggest that civilization was traveling with them, not after them. He intercepted groups of finely bedecked tourists spending the day at a scenic spot, the land having become "enjoyable."

Grabill undoubtedly was among the photographers who rushed to Wounded Knee in December, 1890, as soon as news of the tragedy was heard. No photographer had been present when the fight erupted—it was over before anyone knew how it had begun—but within minutes the ground was strewn with unknown numbers of wounded and more than 150 dead Sioux (including women and children), as well as 25 dead and 39 wounded soldiers.

Snow was in the air, so the Indian bodies had been abandoned where they fell to be blanketed in white. When photographers arrived at the scene a few days later they captured the grisly spectacle—bodies frozen in grotesque positions, or piled on a wagon, or lying in a tangled heap before consignment to a gaping grave. A reporter on the scene noted that although the photographers were the last to leave the field, they could not fully depict with a camera what had happened at Wounded Knee. As Black Elk, a survivor, summarized: "I did not know then how much was ended. When I look back now

142.   "VILLA OF BRULE." 1891

from this high hill of my old age, I can still see the butchered women and children lying heaped and scattered all along the crooked gulch as plain as when I saw them with eyes still young. And I can see that something else died there in the bloody mud, and was buried in the blizzard. A people's dream died there."[2]

Grabill's most compelling portrayal of the last frontier is a series of photographs, few in number, of the Indian-military relationship. In the cold January air of 1891 the photographer set up his camera at the Pine Ridge Agency. The group of Indians and soldiers who together faced his lens was barely removed in time or place from Wounded Knee. He photographed the gathering and the seemingly halcyon days that followed. His image of the Indian tipis stretching in lyric patterns across what seems to be free space belies the tenor of the times. His finely composed photograph with clusters of ponies watering in the foreground evokes serenity and timelessness. One feels that life for the Indian was yet measured in cycles of suns and moons.

Both photography and the West underwent vast changes in the generation from 1865 to 1890: the photographic process gathered speed and the settling of the West gathered momentum. New technologies thrust photography into the modern age with techniques for mass-production and standardization of equipment and materials, while industrialization laid the West bare to civilizing forces.

In that single generation, such rapid growth and expansion took place that few had time for reflection. Events continually altered the western spaces, and new figures and relationships emerged with such suddenness that even to those who lived in the period the frontier seemed a fleeting dream. Photographers and settlers were caught up in the excitement of the times, trying simply to seize each moment.

By today's standards photography and the West were primitives, but their age of innocence was rapidly ending.

NOTES

1. *Sturgis Weekly Record* (South Dakota), 26 November 1886.

2. Quoted in Dee Brown, *Bury My Heart at Wounded Knee* (New York: Holt, Rinehart & Winston, 1970), p. 446.

357. "We have It Rich." Washing and
panning gold. Rockerville. Dak.
Old timers. Spriggs. Lamb and Dillon at work.
Photo and copyright by Grabill, 1889.

143. "WE HAVE IT RICH." WASHING AND PANNING GOLD, ROCKERVILLE, DAKOTA. OLD TIMERS, SPRIGGS, LAMB AND DILLON AT WORK. 1889

144. VIEWING HOSTILE INDIAN CAMP. 1891

145.   INDIAN CHIEFS AND U.S. OFFICIALS. TAKEN AT PINE RIDGE. JANUARY 16, 1891

146. DEVIL'S TOWER FROM WEST SIDE SHOWING MILLIONS OF TONS OF FALLEN ROCK. TOWER 800 FEET HIGH, FROM ITS BASE

147. "SPEARFISH FALLS." OUR FRIENDS, THERE. JUNE 22, 1890

148.   CORPORAL PAUL WERNERT AND GUNNERS OF BATTERY "E" 1ST ARTILLERY. 1891

Photo and copyright by Grabill, '91.
Deadwood, S. D.

149.   THE GREAT HOSTILE CAMP. 1891

220

150.   GENERAL MILES AND STAFF. 1891

151.   Adam Clark Vroman, PREPARING FOR THE ASCENT OF MESA ENCANTADA, DETAIL

The Romantic West

Photographically speaking, the West as subject matter had engaged the lens as a place in the years of exploration, and then as an event in the settling years. In the 1890s, contained and subdued by civilizing forces, the West presented itself as an idea. The Census Bureau Report issued in 1890 officially declared that the frontier as a place had ended, and a few years later the young historian Frederick Jackson Turner neatly consigned the frontier as a force to historical memory. True or not, new ideas about the land and the West were rapidly gaining credence. The philosophy of such men as Thoreau reached a national audience and the voice of John Muir began to pick up echoes and reverberations in the land as he spoke to an audience that looked to the wilderness from suburban safety rather than from a wilderness clearing.

Photography, like the frontier, had undergone a rapid transformation. When Turner propounded his frontier thesis in 1893, photographs had changed from a pioneer effort to a sophisticated system. The evolution had essentially taken place in the space of a decade, and its beginning could be said to date to 1883, when George Eastman built his first factory for the large-scale production of photographic materials. Developments and improvements in process and equipment followed in rapid succession, and as others invented or discovered processes or formulas, George Eastman perfected the manufacturing and marketing techniques that made them commercially successful. Inventors might possess the patents on materials and processes, but Eastman's patents covered the methods and machinery of production. His became by far the most important name in innovation.

With the perfection of machinery to coat both glass and paper with gelatin emulsions, it was but a short step for the industrial genius to extend the process to printing papers. The T. C. Roche Company had patented the bromide process, but Eastman's expertise made bromide-coated paper a commercial success. As early as 1884, he began production.

Bromide paper, in contrast to albumen, was a developing-out paper, which means that the image "developed" by chemical means rather than printing-out in the sun. Developing-out papers offered marked advantage over printing-out albumen paper:

1. They required an exposure of only ten to forty seconds, and could use artificial light;

2. Prints could be manipulated during exposure or development, giving the photographer far more control;

3. Enlargements were now practical, owing to the increased speed;

4. Bromide could be coated on a variety of paper surfaces, and came ready to use.

Improvements in film made bromide papers even more attractive. Dr. Hermann Vogel discovered the means by which emulsions could be made sensitive to the yellow-green spectrum of light, and thus the photographic rendering of tones in monochrome was greatly improved.

Equipment design had also advanced. The separation of the plateholder from the camera, made possible with the dry plate, developed into the changeable magazine, and the idea of the roll holder came into use with Eastman's paper-backed film. For years researchers had been seeking to replace glass with a flexible support for film emulsion; here again, George Eastman merely put the experiments of others into a practical and usable design. From these innovations—plate to roll holder and glass to paper—one of the most far-reaching revolutions in photography that had yet been seen emerged: the Kodak system of photography. With his genius for rearrangement and refabrication—he loaded the roll holder with enough film for one hundred exposures and placed it inside the camera—George Eastman announced in his first Kodak Instruction Booklet:[1]

To-day photography has been reduced to a cycle of three simple operations: 1.—Pull the String. 2.—Turn the Key. 3.—Press the Button. This is the essence of photography and the greatest improvement of them all; for where practice of the art was formerly confined to those who could give it study and time and room, it is now feasible for *everybody*. THE KODAK CAMERA RENDERS POSSIBLE THE KODAK SYSTEM, whereby the mere mechanical act of taking the picture, which anybody can perform, is *divorced* from all the chemical manipulations of preparing and finishing pictures which only experts can perform. Hence it is now easy for any person of ordinary intelligence to learn to take good photographs in ten minutes.

Once the hundred exposures were made the "photographer" sent the whole apparatus, weighing about a pound and a half, to a dealer, who unloaded the exposed film, reloaded with a new spool, and developed and processed the owner's pictures. The original investment was twenty-five dollars, with a ten-dollar charge for processing, printing, and reloading. Within a year Eastman introduced a transparent roll film of nitrocellulose, and within the next few years daylight-loading film. The man from Rochester had not simply replaced glass with a flexible film support, he had lifted the responsibility and knowledge from the individual practitioner and placed it on industrial shoulders.

The Kodak concept of photography created an entirely new class of picture-maker, with implications not only for the professional but for the serious amateur as well. Manufacturers quickly capitalized on the fact that photography, once an individual pursuit, was now big business, and incredible advances in equipment and materials for the serious amateur developed concurrently with—perhaps because of—the Kodak system. The focal plane shutter, located directly in front of the dry plate, was introduced commercially in Germany by C. P. Goerz in 1890. In that year the Carl Zeiss firm perfected the manufacture of the anastigmat lens, which brought sharp definition to the edge of the image; double anastigmats quickly followed, the first produced in 1892.

While the decade of the dry plate gave rise to nearly double the number of professional photographers, as well as nearly eighty amateur societies, the Kodak put 50,000 "photographers" on the scene almost overnight. At the same time an equally important industrial and technical advance thrust photography itself into a new role. This was the development of the modern method by which the reproduction of halftone illustrations became practical and accurate. By the mid-nineties the photograph became a daily reality for the public in two basic forms: as reproductions in magazines, newspapers, and books, and as snapshots. The photographic print as a salable commodity, in and for itself, became largely a thing of the past. The effect on the photographers who continued to rely on selling prints was immediate. Other professionals realized that the major avenue for selling one's work led to the publishing houses, and William H. Jackson and L. A. Huffman set their courses in that direction.

More than threatening the portrait and view business of the heretofore professional, the new role of the photograph as mass-produced and reproduced image challenged the very philosophy and idea of the photographic art. Serious image-makers had to seek new meanings and make further claims for their work. So it was predictable, if not entirely desirable, that photographers came under the influence of painting. It had happened in England a few years earlier when the professionals, pressed to dis-

tinguish themselves as the amateur and commercial uses of photography grew, began to emulate painting. American photographers, too, now looked to other arts—handcrafts and painting—seeking to turn the camera into an art machine to which artistic expression could be applied.

At precisely the time that a major breakthrough had been made in lenses—and orthochromatic emulsions and higher-speed films made a sharp, crisp image possible—many photographers began to employ "impressionistic" soft-focus techniques. With soft-focus lenses they obliterated textures and produced fuzzy backgrounds and blank skies. New, faster papers rendered a longer tonal range and sharper images, yet photographers turned to the murky, subdued tones of the typical painter's palette of the period. Edward Sheriff Curtis used gold toner on rough-surfaced paper, while others applied brown (sepia) tone to the prints. In varying ways and degrees photographers applied their hand to the print itself. Among the most successful (but now obscure) photographers of his day was Carl Moon. An examination of his negatives reveals that he cropped nearly every one, selected out in his enlarger, retouched heavily, and drew on the finished print. He later painted his photographs in the belief that "a collection that would combine both photographic accuracy and careful color in a permanent medium would possess greater future value than a collection in monotone alone could possess."[2] It was considered complimentary when a reviewer wrote that photographs "didn't look like photographs."

As for the West, with increasing accessibility it became ever more familiar and popular as a pictorial subject. People bought books and postcards of it and made snapshots of themselves there.

For professional field photographers to survive in the mid-nineties a new photographic purpose had to be found. In search of a subject, photographers rediscovered the West in the form of its aboriginal and Spanish inhabitants.

The Indian particularly had been of photographic interest since the first image-makers came upon him, but largely as a curiosity. Now photographers turned to the native Americans for those elements of ethnological, artistic, and photographic significance they could lend the photographic medium.

The advances in photography that had occurred by the year 1900 were enormous, but photography was, after all, still a frontier medium largely without a tradition. Photography was then barely sixty years of age and its intrinsic worth and meaning had as yet only begun to be probed, particularly in the West.

NOTES

1. Carl W. Ackerman, *George Eastman* (Boston: Houghton Mifflin Co., 1930), p. 78.

2. Carl Moon, "A Brief Account of the Making of this Collection of Indian Pictures," 1923. Carl Moon papers, Huntington Library, San Marino, California.

THE PICTORIAL WEST: CHARLES F. LUMMIS (1859–1928)

The West as place had become familiar to the American people when a voice with a distinctly eastern accent began to extol another of its aspects. It belonged to Charles Fletcher Lummis, who suggested a new attitude toward the Spanish and Indian cultures, largely ignored in the rush to "civilization."

Lummis, a Yankee by birth and boyhood, had early glimpses of the West through the novels of Mayne Reid—who used the Southwest as background for his stories—but Lummis had yet to see the West firsthand when he entered Harvard as a freshman in 1877.[1] At Harvard, Charles, like his classmate and friend Theodore Roosevelt, undertook a rigorous physical program, for each had been an undersized, frail child, and they shared a need to prove themselves physically. The West became a testing ground for both.

In 1881 Charlie moved to Chillicothe, Ohio—the farthest west he had ever been. He worked for the oldest newspaper west of the Alleghenies, and he also indulged interests in archaeology, hunting, and fishing. His literary bent found early form in a tiny volume of poetry which he printed on birch bark. He sent copies to such notables as Emerson, Whitman, Longfellow—and his long-read favorite, Mayne Reid.

In 1884 Lummis struck a bargain with Colonel Harrison Gray Otis of the *Los Angeles Times:* he would walk to California and write a weekly letter for the *Times* if he were paid five dollars per letter and, at the end of the 3,000-mile journey, were given a job with the paper. Hidden in the deal, though he did not know it, was a renunciation of his Yankee life and a commitment to the West for the rest of his days.

His trek began, and he wrote of his adventures and misadventures. When he arrived in New Mexico he knew he had come home. "Once I had reached Spanish America and the hearts of its people, I realized that this was where I belonged."[2] And as he walked, Lummis's vision filled with the beauty of the West itself: "The World's Wonderland is not in Europe, not in Egypt, not in Asia, but in the West of our own United States. Area for area no other land on earth is half so crowded with marvels of the first magnitude and of such range—of antiquities, scenery, anthropology and picturesqueness in every sort."[3]

The day after arriving in Los Angeles he went to work. He seemed to thrive on it, and drove himself like a man possessed. At the same time he explored the southern California area. When the Apache wars again broke out Lummis grabbed the opportunity to return to the Southwest as a war correspondent. He stayed three months, living with the scouts and soldiers at the front.

During his years in Los Angeles he strengthened his ties to the Spanish people and their culture. He became a frequent visitor to Rancho Camulos, the setting for

152. CROSS OF THE PENITENTE. 1888

Helen Hunt Jackson's novel *Ramona*, and in 1888 Lummis published a small booklet of ten copyrighted photographs that proved that the setting was just as she had described it.[4]

At the age of twenty-eight Lummis suffered a stroke. Partly paralyzed and with his speech gone, he turned to his Spanish friends in the Southwest. He arrived there in February, 1888, and began a diary that he kept for the next forty years.

Fully planning to return to the *Times* as soon as possible, he continued his journalistic pursuits. As he explored the cultural traditions and sites of America's oldest settlements, he sought documentation for future references. He bought a 5-by-8 camera with a Dallmeyer lens which he could operate although his left arm was paralyzed. It was difficult enough to manipulate the view camera, but, Lummis wrote:[5]

It was even harder to do my developing. But I made in this time many thousands of 5×8 plates, developed them and made my blue prints. For silver prints I had to take my negatives to Albuquerque.

If there is anything that is something of a test, it is to develop two 5×8 glass negatives at a time in an adobe room with a big basin bowl for a sink, no outlet except the outside door, no running water, nor other water except what was brought in tinajas [pottery jars] and without any other facility whatever.

I cut myself pretty badly several times where there were reef edges on the glass—for which my chief concern was that the blood spoiled the negatives. But of that host of pictures made at that time, while nearly all are interesting, there are many that are unique and can never be made again—of types that are dead, buildings that are destroyed, ceremonials that are no more.

Shortly after he took up photography, Lummis made his most unique images. Rumor hinted that the Brothers of the Penitente, a religious order long believed to have disappeared, still existed and carried out their secret rites at Easter. Legend told that the rituals included flagellation with fiber thongs, scourging the body by lying naked on beds of cactus thorns, and even crucifying one of the brothers in re-enactment of the Crucifixion. Few believed this, even fewer spoke of it, but those who did knew that the order would kill anyone who tried to confirm the rumors. Lummis determined that he would not only witness the crucifixion but that he would also photograph it.

On the Thursday before Easter of 1888, with two friends holding six-shooters and Lummis's gun cocked on top of his camera, he approached and made photographs of the procession of the Brothers of the Penitente from the town to the burial ground. There were threats, but he managed to persuade the mayor of the town to allow him to photograph. The following day he set up his camera to record the event:[6]

Two Brothers of Light dug a deep hole on the slope. Beside it they laid a huge cross. Out from the Morada, with a Brother of Light holding each arm, came a fellow naked to the waist. He wore white cotton drawers and a black hangman's cap over his head. In his left side was a bleeding wound down which the blood ran to his feet in a stream two inches wide.

Laying himself down on the cross he was attached there hands and feet with a new half-inch rope which cut into the flesh as each Brother of Light put a foot on him to pull tighter. The cross with its burden was then set up and packed into the hole, and another penitente (similarly marked, with a burro-load of buckthorn cactus strapped tightly on his bare back) came and lay with his feet to the foot of the cross and his head on a stone. Thereat the Hermano Mayor gave me the sign and I made my photographs. They showed the procession forming for the march to the Campo Santo, the self-whippers, the Hermano Mayor and the men carrying on their shoulders the arms of enormous crosses. These dragged ten feet on the ground and were of the calibre of goodly telegraph poles.

Even with the photographic evidence, no magazine in the country would publish the article Lummis wrote; though *Cosmopolitan* finally printed the article, with the photographs, many still disbelieved. True to prediction, however, Lummis nearly paid with his life for these photographs. Hired assassins made several attempts to kill him, and one finally succeeded in unloading eight pieces of buckshot into him.

Still partially paralyzed, the journalist decided to live among the Indians. He moved to Isleta Pueblo, along the Rio Grande, and became an intimate tribal friend, learning both language and cultural practices. As a result of his experiences he became a crusader, taking up the causes of the Spanish American and the Indian, wielding his pen to arouse public opinion against the mistreatment of both peoples.

Into Isleta Pueblo and Lummis's life a solitary figure walked in 1888, a man of extraordinary intellect and curiosity. He was the Swiss-born, multilingual Adolph Bandelier. The enthusiast Lummis and the scientist Bandelier—armed with portfolios of notes, surveying materials, and little else—would travel throughout the Southwest. They covered thousands of miles together, explored and documented ruins, valleys, and canyons, understanding and moving freely among the peoples of that little-known region. When they returned, Lummis settled at Isleta and Bandelier in Santa Fe. Soon the pair headed for the ruins of Peru and Bolivia. Lummis felt honored that Bandelier, the scientific intellect, should invite him along, for it meant that he considered Lummis a competent archaeologist. Lummis carried a 5-by-8 camera, having partially regained the use of his arm, and photographed for over a year while Bandelier kept his careful notes.

When Lummis returned from the expedition in early 1894 he settled in Los Angeles. To make a living he printed some of his photographs and sold part of the collection he had gathered during his years in the Southwest. But he had other, more vital preoccupations than making a living. He became involved in an effort to save the Franciscan missions by organizing the Landmarks Club, the first of its kind in the United States. At the same time he took over the editorship of *Land of Sunshine*, a twenty-four-page tourist-oriented publication. In Lummis's hands the pamphlet evolved into a first-rate magazine that promoted the entire Southwest, a term which, in fact, he coined. His publication attracted a considerable following in the East, as well as locally.

Theodore Roosevelt reportedly told him: "I want you to know that I always read the *Land of Sunshine* though it is the only magazine I have time to read now." Though Roosevelt may have exaggerated, it is certain that upon becoming President he asked Lummis to come to Washington, seeking the advice of his Harvard acquaintance on the status of the Indian. Lummis helped to prepare the background paper for Roosevelt's Indian policy. And, all the while, Lummis was writing books about the area.

Charles Lummis tried many things in his life—and journalism and photography were two of his useful tools. Throughout his career he photographed with a plate camera and processed his own work, often using blueprint paper because it was inexpensive. (He shared his blueprint formula with William Henry Jackson in 1899, as well as a fine "California dinner" for which he also was noted.)

Lummis's photographs do not indicate artistic sensitivity, but rather a journalistic acumen. He considered his photographs useful documents, and wrote of them: "Probably in the last thirty-eight years I have made more five-by-eight negatives of the Southwest than any one else. I could lavishly illustrate a score of volumes like this from my own photographs. But I care less—and the reader not at all—whether the illustration is by me or by another, so that it shall be the best. I did not always get the best picture of everything—and I am glad to make room for my betters. My idea of illustrations in a book like this is that they should really ILLUSTRATE—that they answer the questions the text provokes."[7]

He was among the first photographers to live with the Southwest Indians, to gather their legends and songs, to photograph their ceremonies, and to convince them that the photographic shutter was not, in fact, an "evil eye." Charles Lummis promoted the idea of the Southwest among the southern Californians and, in truth, paved an attractive path for others to follow, particularly other photographers. They could board the Santa Fe train in Pasadena or Los Angeles and be in Albuquerque the following morning, to begin a journey to the pueblos and the land made exotic and wonderful, in part, by the pen of Lummis and others whom he published.

At a time when New Englanders increasingly fled to Europe or the Far East, Lummis saw within America the cultural riches and natural beauty these travelers sought. He devoted himself to the task of bringing to the attention of Americans the heritage which lay in their own enormous backyard; he created, in effect, a new image of the West. Perhaps Douglas Fairbanks summed it up when he wrote in Lummis's house book, "There are certain men who are as vital as our Frontier."

NOTES

1. Biographical information on Charles Fletcher Lummis is taken from Turbese Lummis Fiske and Keith Lummis, *Charles F. Lummis: The Man and His West* (Norman: University of Oklahoma Press, 1975), and Dudley Gordon, *Crusader in Corduroy* (Los Angeles: Cultural Assets Press, 1972).

2. Fiske and Lummis, *op. cit.*, pp. 20–21.

3. Ibid., p. 25.

4. Charles F. Lummis, *The Home of Ramona* (Los Angeles: Chas. F. Lummis & Co., 1888). He copyrighted the photographs of "Camulos, the fine old Spanish Estate described by Mrs. Helen Hunt Jackson as the Home of 'Ramona' " in 1887.

5. Fiske and Lummis, *op. cit.*, p. 43.

6. Ibid., p. 45.

7. Charles F. Lummis, *Mesa, Cañon and Pueblo* (New York: Century Co., 1925), p. ix.

153. PENITENTE WITH SANTOS. 1888

154. CRUCIFIXION CEREMONY OF THE PENITENTE. 1888

234

155. PROCESSION OF THE PENITENTE. 1888

A WANTING TO SEE FELLOW:
ADAM CLARK VROMAN
(1856–1916)

Adam Clark Vroman was one of the many people whom Charles Lummis influenced. In 1892 Vroman and his wife traveled West from Illinois for her health, and settled in Pasadena. Though Esther Vroman died soon after, her husband chose to remain, and he opened a bookstore in 1894.[1]

It was Lummis who first interested Vroman in photography, late in 1894. Vroman adopted a fairly sophisticated system that had been developed, essentially, within one decade, and while his store became one of the first Kodak agencies in the area, Vroman himself, perhaps following the lead of Lummis, used a 6 1/2-by-8 1/2 camera.

Describing himself as a "general 'wanting to see' fellow,"[2] he made his first trip to the Southwest in the summer of 1895, with the purpose of viewing the Hopi Snake Dance. He traveled with a group of local people, among them the passionate collector Mrs. T. S. C. Lowe, Mr. H. N. Rust, also a collector, and a Mr. C. J. Crandall, "a professional photographer (and the man to whom I go for advice, when in trouble, photographically)."[3]

The party boarded the train in Pasadena and by the following morning had hired a wagon to head north from Holbrook for the pueblo, planning to camp along the way. Vroman apparently had never camped before, but he adjusted to the food and way of life, and in his neat,

back-slanted hand he described the journey and made photographs as he went along.

When Vroman's group arrived at the foot of the mesa they found about forty others encamped. The party decided to go to the top of the mesa and the Indian pueblo, though it was not an easy proposition; the problem was "how to get Mrs. Lowe to top. 600 feet almost perpendicular wall of rock to climb and Mrs. Lowe weighing 260 almost helpless as to walking and trail steep enough for any one good at climbing."[4] They engaged several Indians to bear Mrs. Lowe to the top on a litter, and the intrepid lady was photographed by Vroman and Crandall as the ascent began. Once there, the photographers explored the surroundings with their cameras. It is difficult to know which photographs are Vroman's and which are Crandall's, for they shared viewpoints and a sense of camaraderie, and the same photographs are found in both collections.

On the day of the Snake Dance, Vroman positioned his camera early in the morning, "in readiness an hour before Dance was to commence as well as probably a dozen other 'camerasts.'" The Snake Dance commenced just before sunset, so the light was not good for photography, and of course the dancers were in motion, so all "camerasts" experienced the same difficulties. But Vroman noted on his photographs: "Am told by parties

156. "OUR HOME ON THE MESA." LEFT TO RIGHT: MRS. LOWE, CRANDALL, RUST, VROMAN, AND MONTOYA. 1895

who have seen other views made at same time, that the ones I made are most successful of any, so in that much I am pleased?" [question mark his]

The bookseller-photographer came away from his first southwestern experience highly impressed: "My first thought after it was all over was to see it again and know more about it, why it was and how it is planned. I felt I could spend a year right there, be one of them and learn their ways and beliefs." After three nights on the mesa, the group returned to Holbrook, and the following morning set out to see the Petrified Forest. They arrived in late afternoon at the "forest." Vroman made some photographs but wrote in his diary: "To show in a satisfactory manner this wonderful freak of nature is difficult, the one thing lacking in photography, *Color* is so important."

On one of the last evenings by the campfire, the group mused over what their friends in Pasadena would say if they could see them "just as we were." Vroman produced some flash powder, which he and Crandall had also used for the indoor shots at the pueblo; they rigged a fuse by soaking string in bacon fat with one end in the powder, and the campfire scene returned with them to Pasadena.

Vroman and a group of companions planned to return to the Southwest to witness the Snake Dance and to visit some of the Zuñi pueblos in 1897. In contrast to his previous trip, Vroman recorded that "nearly 200 white people saw the dance, 3 times the number of '95."[5] Again, a number of photographers attended the ceremony, Vroman later noting: "Mr. Hayt and Mr. Munson [sic] both were so wrapped up in watching the Dancers that they forgot all about their cameras and at one time I had seven cameras to work from my point of view. I hope they may all turn out well."

From that initial meeting, Vroman observed, "Mr. Munson [spelled according to pronunciation] proved a valuable member of the party a man of intelligence and a student in Ethnology and enjoyed the trip to its full, I believe." A close friendship evolved between Frederick Monsen and Vroman.

Vroman and Hayt planned to see the Grand Canyon on this trip and to visit some of the Zuñi pueblos. As they prepared to leave for Laguna pueblo they met Dr. Frederick W. Hodge of the Bureau of American Ethnology. The doctor had assembled a small party, planning to scale the Enchanted Mesa or Katzimo, to confirm that it had been the site of the precursor to the present pueblo at Acoma. The pair joined Hodge and with the aid of preconstructed ladders, ropes, and not a little courage, the group scaled the 431-foot wall, finding proof of previous habitation. Lummis, who had first printed the Indian version of the story, wrote in October, 1897, that Vroman's "Deadly photograph is in evidence,"[6] leaving no doubt. Hodge had been fortunate to have the photographer along and wrote, "Vroman was a good traveller and superb photographer. . . . His only shortcoming was a complete lack of sense of direction. He used to set up his tripod in the midst of Juniper and piñon stands, walk away a short distance to see if he could get a better shot of Acoma, for example, and then become lost. I was always having to find his tripod for him!"[7]

The following year Vroman and a group of three Pasadena businessmen who shared mutual interests formed a club. The group is pictured at the Mission San Juan Capistrano (all in their business suits, and wearing ties and stiff collars), and on Sunday outings in the Arroyo Seco in Pasadena, tripods and dry-plate cameras in tow. It is evident from Vroman's albums that he enjoyed photographing his companions and the event of travel as much as other subject matter.[8] He made several trips with friends and other photographers, particularly Frederick Monsen; it is not known if Vroman ever made photographic excursions alone.

Monsen shared his interest in ethnology, and each became involved in making an authentic record of the Indian. They were not competitive but mutually supportive. As Vroman and other serious photographers noted, it became increasingly difficult to obtain a subject, with snapshooters paying Indians to pose or else frightening them away. Once a group of photographers found a willing Indian for the kind of photograph they wanted, they set up one camera and each, in turn, made a negative for his own purpose, from the same viewpoint. A portrait of a young Indian girl, posed against the same background with the same light, is found in the collections of Vroman, Monsen, P. G. Gates, and C. J. Crandall. Close examination reveals slight variations in the position of the hand or head or eye movement, confirming the working procedure.[9]

Vroman's last trip to the Southwest apparently was in 1904. A photograph taken of him standing by his mule in Canyon de Chelly holding a Kodak (perhaps the influence of his friend Monsen) shows him with a scarf about his neck, but still very much the proper gentleman in his business suit. Unlike Lummis, Adam Clark Vroman's life-style had been little changed by his southwestern encounters, and after that time his interests and inquisitive nature led him into other pursuits so that photography, too, became secondary. He was, truly, a "wanting to see fellow," and once he had seen he moved on. He made several trips to Japan and gathered a sizable collection of Japanese ivory and wood carvings. He took a camera on these trips, but it is obvious that he did so to take snapshots rather than serious pictures.

Adam Clark Vroman embodied the serious amateur who was beginning to appear on the American scene. He took up photography as a source of personal enjoyment and satisfaction. He rarely enlarged his photographs but made crisp, meticulous contact prints on platinum paper for his albums. There is no evidence that Vroman considered his photography as other than a personal pleasure, with the exception of his Indian photographs, which he also believed to be of value as ethnological studies. He copyrighted forty-two of these images and gave several hundred prints to the Bureau of American Ethnology. He is not known, however, to have shown his pictures in exhibitions of any kind, nor to have had any artistic pretensions about his photographic work.

Vroman was a cultured man and he cultivated many interests throughout his life, of which photography was but one. Because he never remarried comradeship was important, and he had many friends. His bookstore (in existence today) was akin to a family concern.

Shortly before his death in 1916 the bookseller-photographer sent for the librarian of the Pasadena Public Library to announce the bequest to the library of his collection of books pertaining to California and the Pacific Southwest. In addition, Vroman gave the library ten thousand dollars to supplement the collection, "together with a number of bound albums of photographs many of which," he hastened to add, "I have taken myself."

NOTES

1. Vroman had spent his first thirty-six years in Illinois, working for seventeen years as a railroad agent for the Burlington Railway. John Steven McGroarty, *History of Los Angeles County* (New York: American History Society, Inc., 1923), pp. 412–14.

2. Diary of Adam Clark Vroman, summer, 1895. Vroman Photographic Collection, Huntington Library, San Marino, California.

3. Vroman wrote the account of his first southwestern trip on the back of a series of nineteen photographs taken on the outing. Vroman Photographic Collection, Huntington Library.

4. Vroman diary, summer, 1895. Vroman Photographic Collection, Huntington Library. The quotes concerning the 1895 excursion are taken from this diary.

5. Diary of Adam Clark Vroman, 1897. The author is indebted to Mr. William G. Webb, who generously lent his copy of this diary; the original is privately owned. Quotes concerning the 1897 trip are taken from this diary.

6. Charles F. Lummis, "Hic Jacet Libbey," *Land of Sunshine* 7 (1897): 249.

7. Lawrence Clark Powell, "Photographer of the Southwest," *Westways* (1958), p. 13.

8. He gave sixteen albums of photographs to the Pasadena Public Library.

9. See, for example, Walter Hough, *The Hopi Indian* (Iowa: Torch Press, 1915), for photographs by P. G. Gates that are similar to the work of Vroman and Monsen.

157. CAMINO DEL PADRE, ACOMA PUEBLO. 1902

158.   WEAVING A NAVAJO BLANKET. 1901

159.   GATHERING SNAKES AT THE END OF THE SNAKE CEREMONY. 1897

160.   INDIAN WITH DISPLAY OF POTS AT ACOMA PUEBLO

161.　PREPARING FOR THE ASCENT OF MESA ENCANTADA

162. AROUND THE CAMP FIRE (FLASH LIGHT 10 P.M.). LEFT TO RIGHT: NEPHEW OF OLD ADAMS, VROMAN, OLD ADAMS, MRS. LOWE, RUST, AND CRANDALL. 1895

163. BREAKFAST OUTSIDE HOLBROOK. 1895

WITH A KODAK IN THE LAND OF THE NAVAJO: FREDERICK I. MONSEN (1865–1929)

Frederick Monsen, a Norwegian emigrant, grew up in the West. He was a many-sided, multi-talented man. He and his father worked as a photographic team for the Denver and Rio Grande Railroad when Frederick was but a teenager, having learned the collodion process. The family at one point formed a stock company that toured the Southwest, and Monsen, also very good at sketching, earned his living as an artist on occasion.[1]

For Monsen, photography was only a means by which he could indulge and support his adventurous spirit. With camera in hand he could live a nomadic existence, accepting photographic assignments that took him all over the West as photojournalist for newspapers or on assignment for other photographers (he worked for William H. Jackson, among others).

In the mid-eighties Monsen covered a vast amount of western territory simply by attaching himself to any group that was in the area at the time. Though not listed as an official member of these parties, it is known that he photographed for the geological survey on the boundary between the United States and Mexico in 1886; that he worked for Generals Crook and Miles at the end of the Apache campaign; and that he substituted for the official photographer Frank Nims on the Brown-Stanton survey when Nims broke his leg. In 1891 he joined an expedi-

tion to the Salton Sea and explored lower California, Death Valley, and various other deserts.

In 1893 he began to lecture, his first series devoted to Death Valley and the desert areas, but he still could not settle down. He was listed as "artist and topographer" on the 1896 Yosemite National Park Survey.

As the years passed Monsen worked with smaller and smaller cameras: "After several years of . . . slavery [18×22] I changed to a 14×17 camera, with which I labored for a year or two, when I purchased an 11×14 instrument and soon afterward an 8×10. And so I went merrily on, my cameras growing smaller and my labor less, and so secured a 5×7 camera."[2]

Monsen first went among the Indian tribes of the Southwest in 1894–95 in the capacity of artist, and from 1897 continued to return, sometimes in the company of Vroman, each man making his own photographs of the Indian for his own purposes. Monsen photographed with the intent of illustrating his lectures, while Vroman made authentic documents for his own interest. Neither man was innovative nor sought self-expression.

Vroman made contact prints on platinum paper for his albums, but Monsen began to make enlargements, for he found that a small negative (four by five inches) yielded the kind of print that he wanted. It was not long

164. YANABA, FIVE-YEAR-OLD NAVAJO BLANKET WEAVER, ARIZONA

before the Kodak became his choice. "Certain dyed-in-the-wool opinions advanced by professional friends, that the Kodak was but a toy, and worthless for serious work, only made me more determined to try for myself."[3] Monsen, competent after years of photographic discipline as well as skilled in compositional techniques, found the Kodak a long-awaited dream: "My first Kodak was a revelation. I found myself in possession of an instrument that not only dispensed with ground glass, plateholders, and tripod altogether, but could be used instantaneously, and was ever ready for action, with a roll of films to back it that made it as effective as a magazine rifle. This new order of things proved to be a great blessing for before I had found this new way—the Kodak way—I had never made the kind of Indian picture I wanted."[4]

Monsen established a studio in San Francisco in which an enlarger—purportedly the largest on the West Coast at the time—was mounted on a ceiling track projecting onto the far wall. With this he produced enlargements of all sizes, some larger than twenty by twenty-four inches, which he placed on even larger mats. He began to compile his collection of ethnographic studies of the Southwest Indians while lecturing and making large prints for sale, his sons helping to hand-color the lantern slides.

Like Watkins and countless other victims, Monsen watched his life's work go up in the flames that followed the San Francisco earthquake of 1906. He saved a trunk of lantern slides and prints that were packed in readiness for a lecture tour, buried another in the yard, and fled. Since he was half Watkins's age, he was able to reconstruct his collection partially from prints he had sold or given to various institutions, and his friend Vroman was of considerable aid; he lent Monsen negatives and prints that were Monsen's, as well as some of his own to round out the collection.

Monsen now turned almost exclusively to lecturing. In January, 1907, an exhibition of his prints appeared in New York, followed by several other shows in the East. His work attracted a great deal of attention, the art critic of the *New York Evening Post* (7 April) concluding: "I did not think it possible to put so much art in photography. I can't understand how you succeeded in getting such immensely artistic effects with a Kodak, when the 'camera' people are doing so much more talking and producing so much less." His lectures received even more exuberant praise. Monsen's talent for oratory and drama, his sense of humor and anecdote, his broadness of experience and interest made him a sought-after lecturer. He charmed ladies' club audiences and impressed scientific ones. He went before geographical, archaeological, and historical societies and was received at Harvard and Columbia.

Eadweard Muybridge had caused a sensation with his lifesize projections of figures in motion; Monsen's exquisitely painted colorgraphs caused the same breathtaking effect, for they predated color photography. Thomas Moran, whose study of Turner's use of light and color made him a critical viewer, commented: "If it were possible for us artists to produce with pigment on canvas what Monsen creates with color and light, what a wonderful achievement it would be!"[5]

Monsen lived part of the year at the Explorers Club in New York and the rest in Pasadena, and continued to travel to the Southwest. His trips did not go unnoticed. On 17 December 1907 George Eastman wrote him: "If I had not planned to go to Europe this spring I would ask you to let me go along with you on your western trip. If you have to go the following year please bear me in mind. I would be glad to pay all expenses of the trip and your time besides for the privilege of going with you."[6] Two years later Monsen and Eastman did journey to the Southwest, and the grateful industrialist thanked him, saying: "I therefore venture to enclose a check for five hundred dollars and ask you to accept it with my best wishes."[7]

Monsen sold his colorgraphs all over the world, and in 1923 Henry Huntington bought nine portfolios, consisting of 373 large photographic prints. Monsen's main income continued to derive from these sources as well as from lecturing throughout the first two decades of the twentieth century. He described himself as explorer, geographer, ethnographer, artist, adventurer, lecturer, and photographer.

Monsen welcomed the Kodak as an art machine, and that was the way he sought to employ it. His photographs are well composed, revealing an innate artistic sense of significant form, and a perceptive eye. They are fine pictorial representations of the Indian as the white man sought to portray him—he shows sunlit bronzed bodies with no flesh tones, and conveys the atmosphere of the environment rather than its harsh reality. With his camera he painted the Indian as the "Arab of the Southwest," picturesque and colorful. In their day his were considered fine photographs, truly the best that the camera could produce.

Monsen typified the attitude toward nature and art at the beginning of the twentieth century. It would not be until a body of work had been produced with which comparisons could be made, and by which standards could be set, that a new aesthetic of photography in the West would emerge.

NOTES

1. Although he was concertmaster of the Norwegian National Theater orchestra and a foremost comedian in Norway, Monsen's father listed his occupation as "photographer" when he entered the United States in 1868. Frederick's mother had been an Ibsen ingenue in the avant-garde theater, and the couple lavished upon their only son the benefits of their background. From private communication with Christina Wilkinson, great-granddaughter of Frederick I. Monsen, who generously shared her research material and notes on the photographer with the author.

2. Frederick I. Monsen, *With a Kodak in the Land of the Navajo* (Rochester, N.Y.: Eastman Kodak Co., n.d.), pp. 18–19. This booklet is believed to have been written by Monsen, at Eastman's request, shortly after Monsen's return from the Southwest with George Eastman in 1909.

3. Ibid., p. 20.

4. Ibid.

5. *The Frederick Monsen Ethnographic Indian Photographs* (New York: Explorers Club, n.d.), p. 4.

6. Eastman to Monsen, 17 December 1907. George Eastman papers, George Eastman House, Rochester, N.Y.

7. Eastman to Monsen, 23 September 1909. George Eastman papers.

165.   MOHAVE INDIANS

166.   NAVAJO BOY FROM MONUMENT VALLEY, ARIZONA

167.   NAVAJO INDIANS, ARIZONA. LITTLE NAVAJO SHEEP HERDER

168. POPOMANA, HOPI MAIDEN OF SHONGOPOVI, PAINTED DESERT, ARIZONA

169. KAUWENA, THE OLDEST WOMAN IN WALPI. THERE ARE FOUR GENERATIONS BETWEEN THE OLD WOMAN AND THE CHILD

170. A LITTLE ARISTOCRAT. CHILD OF TECHUNUVA, CHIEF OF THE
VILLAGE OF ORAIBI

171. THE DAUGHTER OF THE GOVERNOR OF ISLETA,
VICENTE JIRON. 1890

172. HOPI BOYS PLAYING ON THE VERY EDGE OF THE MESA WHERE A MISSTEP WOULD MEAN A FALL OF SEVERAL
HUNDRED FEET TO THE ROCKS BELOW

CHRONOLOGY

1829   Carleton E. Watkins born in New York
1830   Eadweard Muybridge born in Kingston-on-Thames, England
        Andrew J. Russell born in New York
1836   William S. Soule born in Maine
1839   Louis-Jacques-Mandé Daguerre announces discovery of his process in January, but does not reveal the nature of daguerreotypy until August 19
        First printed account of Daguerre's technique arrives in New York on September 20—beginning of photography in America
1840s   Scovill Manufacturing Company begins production of silver-plated copper for daguerreotypy
1840   Timothy O'Sullivan born in Ireland
        Joseph Petzval calculates fast lens for portraiture and landscape photography; produced by Voigtländer & Sohn the following year
1841   William A. Bell born in England
        John C. Frémont unsuccessfully attempts to make daguerreotypes on his first western expedition
1843   John K. Hillers born in Germany
        William Henry Jackson born in New York
1844   William Henry Fox Talbot publishes *Pencil of Nature*, first book to be illustrated with actual photographs
1846   A. C. Hull born in Indiana
1847   Edward Anthony becomes supplier of imported daguerreotype materials from France; later manufactures them in U.S.
1849   Camillus S. Fly born in Missouri
        Carleton E. Watkins sails for California
        Langenheim Brothers introduce photography on albumenized glass in U.S.
        History and Practice of the Art of Photography, first bound book on the subject in U.S., published
1850   First issue of *Daguerreian Journal* appears
        Langenheim Brothers introduce stereoscopic views on glass in Philadelphia; initially not very successful
1851   Eadweard Muybridge emigrates to America
        Frederick Scott Archer describes thick, gooey liquid as

medium for holding light-sensitive materials on glass—collodion, fastest process yet devised, replaces all others in terms of popular use
        First issue of *Photographic Art Journal* appears
        John Wesley Jones claims to have made 1,500 daguerreotypes along route from San Francisco to Missouri, thus becoming the first to photograph the Rockies (extant drawings made from works; originals lost)
        W. C. Mayhew accompanies Capt. Lorenzo Sitgreaves's expedition for Topographical Corps
1852   John K. Hillers emigrates to New York City
1853   John A. Whipple becomes first commercial wet-plate photographer in U.S.
        Photographic Art Journal publishes paper photographic print of Edward Anthony done by Whipple
        John Mix Stanley accompanies Gov. I. I. Stevens's railway survey and photographs Indians
        Solomon N. Carvalho accompanies Frémont expedition through San Juan Mountains; publishes *Incidents of Travel and Adventure in the Far West* (1857) with illustrations taken from daguerreotypes (originals lost)
1854   Carleton E. Watkins learns daguerreotypy working in Robert Vance's San Jose studio
        L. A. Huffman born in Iowa
        Patents issued to J. A. Cutting for ambrotype and bromide processes
c. 1855 Transition from daguerreotype to wet-collodion process begins
1856   Carleton E. Watkins photographs New Almaden Quicksilver Mine
        Eadweard Muybridge opens bookstore in San Francisco
        Solomon D. Butcher born in West Virginia
        Adam C. Vroman born in Illinois
        Patent issued to H. L. Smith for the tintype, one of the few distinctly American varieties of photographs (also known as ferrotype and melainotype)
1857   Lt. Joseph C. Ives travels by steamer to Black Canyon, head

of navigation on Colorado River; attempts to make photographs but loses equipment in gale; report includes one lithograph derived from a photograph (original lost)

1858   William H. Jackson begins series of jobs as retoucher and colorist in photographic studios

Introduction of collodion and growing interest in the stereograph begin to swell the ranks of amateur photographers

1859   Timothy O'Sullivan works under Alexander Gardner in Mathew Brady's Washington, D.C., gallery

Charles F. Lummis born in Massachusetts

Introduction of cartes de visite, photographs the size of calling cards, in U.S.; in vogue throughout 1860s

Oliver Wendell Holmes publishes "The Stereoscope and the Stereograph" in *Atlantic Monthly*

C. C. Mills accompanies Capt. J. H. Simpson's exploration of Great Basin, Utah

Albert Bierstadt sketches and makes stereoscopic views with Capt. Frederick W. Lander's survey from Puget Sound to South Pass in the Wind River Range, Wyoming

J. D. Hutton accompanies Capt. William F. Raynolds's expedition to region bordering Yellowstone and Missouri rivers, and is perhaps first to photograph Great Falls of the Missouri; Ferdinand V. Hayden in party

1860s Prepared collodion becomes commercially available during the decade

Formation of photographic societies, joined by both professionals and amateurs

1860   Eadweard Muybridge severely wounded in stagecoach accident; returns to England

William H. Jackson learns to process and print photographs in Vermont studio

George Edward Anderson born in Salt Lake City

U.S. Patent Office and other government agencies begin to utilize photography to reproduce drawings

1861   Carleton E. Watkins makes first trip to Yosemite Valley with specially made 18-by-22-inch camera

Englishman Charles Russell devises tannin dry-plate process requiring six times longer exposure than collodion, but plates can be stored several weeks before printing

Coleman Sellers patents the kinematoscope, which simulates motion by revolving photographs

Oliver Wendell Holmes describes simple stereoscope for hand-viewing of stereographs; popularity of stereograph increases

Mathew Brady organizes Photographic Corps to document Civil War; photographers include Alexander Gardner and Timothy O'Sullivan

Timothy O'Sullivan photographs Battle of Bull Run

1862   Timothy O'Sullivan works for Alexander Gardner, photographer for Army of the Potomac

Andrew J. Russell becomes photographer for Military Railroad Construction Corps; maintains only official government photographic laboratory during war

William S. Soule injured at Battle of Antietam

A. C. Hull becomes portraitist in St. Paul gallery

A. A. Forbes born in Wisconsin

1863   Carleton E. Watkins produces enormous album of Yosemite Valley views (prints approximately 16 by 21 inches); selection of his photographs accompanies draft of Yosemite Act to Congress

William H. Jackson returns to Vermont gallery after one year in army

A. C. Hull establishes studio in St. Cloud, Minnesota

The Silver Sunbeam by Dr. John Towler appears at end of year; becomes best-known manual of photography, until end of collodion era; translated into German, French, and Spanish

C. C. Harrison's American-made Globe Lens popularized

Philadelphia Photographer, edited by Edward Wilson, is established (outgrowth of photographic society)

1864   Timothy O'Sullivan photographs aftermath of Battle of Gettysburg

Pres. Abraham Lincoln signs bill (accompanied by Watkins's photographs) making Yosemite Valley a park "for public use, resort and recreation"

1865   Timothy O'Sullivan returns to work in Alexander Gardner's Washington, D.C., gallery after war

Carleton E. Watkins opens Yosemite Art Gallery in San Francisco; photographs published in J. D. Whitney's *Geo-*

logical Survey of California; commissioned to advise Frederick Law Olmsted on preservation and enhancement of Yosemite park; makes first images along Mendocino Coast

William S. Soule opens studio in Chambersburg, Pennsylvania; it burns the following year

L. A. Huffman learns photography in father's shop in Iowa

Frederick I. Monsen born in Norway

Adolph Steinheil produces distortion-free, symmetrical, double objective lens

1866   William H. Jackson heads west

A. C. Hull begins job with E. L. Eaton in Omaha

Carleton E. Watkins meets Clarence King while photographing for California State Survey

Alexander Gardner publishes *Gardner's Photographic Sketch Book of the War*, including forty-two photographs attributed to O'Sullivan

Introduction of cabinet photographs in U.S., similar to cartes de visite but larger

Adolph Steinheil calculates distortion- and color-corrected aplanat lens

1867   Timothy O'Sullivan accompanies King's 40th Parallel Survey; makes images of Virginia City Comstock Lode with burning magnesium wire (first photographs of a mine interior)

William A. Bell accompanies Kansas Pacific Survey group along 32nd Parallel; falls in with Custer's 7th Cavalry campaigning against hostile Indians and obtains first photograph of a massacre victim

Eadweard Muybridge returns to U.S. and begins to document wide range of California life; as "Helios," drives "Flying Studio" to Yosemite, photographing with 6-by-8-inch camera

William S. Soule takes job as clerk at Ft. Dodge; photographs Cheyennes, Arapahoes, Comanches, on own time

A. C. Hull photographs in Colorado, Wyoming, Utah

William H. Jackson takes job in Omaha photographic studio; with brother Edward, later establishes studio "Jackson Brothers, Photographers"

1867–68   Kansas Pacific Railroad Survey (Gen. W. W. Wright, Gen. William J. Palmer)

1867–72   U.S. Geological Exploration of the 40th Parallel (Clarence King)

1867–79   U.S. Geological and Geographical Survey of the Territories (Ferdinand V. Hayden)

1868   Timothy O'Sullivan photographs Snake River and Shoshone Falls with 40th Parallel Survey

William A. Bell finishes with Kansas Pacific Survey and returns to England to compile notes for publication

Carleton E. Watkins wins gold medal for landscape at the Paris Exposition Universelle; fifty Watkins photographs published in J. D. Whitney's *Yosemite Book*; makes first trip to Oregon with painter William Keith

Eadweard Muybridge has twenty of his photographs published in first Yosemite guidebook, *Yosemite: Its Wonders and Its Beauties* by John S. Hittell; accompanies Halleck expedition to Alaska

Andrew J. Russell photographs railway contruction from Cheyenne to Promontory Point, Utah, for Union Pacific Railroad

A. C. Hull works for Jackson Brothers in Omaha

George Robertson works for Alexander Gardner in Washington, D.C.

1869   Meeting of Union Pacific and Southern Pacific railroad construction at Promontory Point, Utah, on May 10—completion of transcontinental railroad

Maj. John Wesley Powell makes first descent of Colorado River; no photographer present

Andrew J. Russell makes famous photographs of joining of the rails at Promontory Point (for years credited to another photographer); fifty Russell photographs published in *The Great West Illustrated*. . . .

William H. Jackson and A. C. Hull travel along just-completed Union Pacific Railroad, making salable views on speculation; meet Ferdinand V. Hayden

Timothy O'Sullivan photographs Salt Lake area, Uintah and Wasatch mountains, before 40th Parallel Survey concludes season in November

William A. Bell publishes *New Tracks in North America*; includes written account of Powell's Colorado River trip

Eadweard Muybridge describes "lateral sky shade" for making cloud and atmospheric effects in *Philadelphia Photographer*;

also mentions special dark cloth with sleeves
William S. Soule works as post photographer at Ft. Sill

1870   Carleton E. Watkins photographs Mt. Lassen and Mt. Shasta on King survey
William H. Jackson becomes official photographer for Hayden survey, unsalaried, but with rights to the survey negatives
Andrew J. Russell has thirty photographs published in Hayden's *Sun Pictures of Rocky Mountain Scenery*
Timothy O'Sullivan accompanies Comm. T. O. Selfridge's expedition to Isthmus of Darien (Panama); relinquishes position to John Moran the following year; photographs appear in *The Three Lakes: Marian, Lall, and Jan, and How They Were Named*, privately published by Clarence King
A. C. Hull leaves Jackson Brothers to set up studio in Nebraska
John K. Hillers resigns from Brooklyn Police Force to accompany ailing brother to California

1871   William H. Jackson explores Yellowstone with Thomas Moran on Hayden survey; becomes known as first photographer of Yellowstone when prints are distributed to Congress
John K. Hillers hired in Santa Fe as crewman for Powell survey
Timothy O'Sullivan accompanies Wheeler survey; first to photograph Grand Canyon (all but a few plates perish in stagecoach mishap)

1871–72   Powell makes second Colorado River expedition

1871–79   U.S. Geographical and Geological Survey of the Rocky Mountain Region (Maj. John Wesley Powell)
U.S. Geographical Surveys West of the 100th Meridian (Lt. George M. Wheeler)

1872   Timothy O'Sullivan joins King survey
Carleton E. Watkins works for King survey, based in California
John K. Hillers becomes photographer-in-chief of Powell survey; photographs mesa country and Paiute Indians
William H. Jackson photographs Grand Teton and Yellowstone on Hayden survey; takes 11-by-14-inch camera into field and devises new dark tent; sells Omaha studio and moves to Washington, D.C., at end of season

Eadweard Muybridge unsuccessfully attempts to photograph Leland Stanford's horses in motion
Creation of Yellowstone National Park

1873   John K. Hillers photographs Glen and Marble canyons, and Zion, Kanab, and Grand canyons on Powell survey
William H. Jackson photographs in Colorado with Hayden survey; makes first photographs of Mount of the Holy Cross; stereo views of Yellowstone published by E. & H. T. Anthony
Timothy O'Sullivan photographs in Southwest with Wheeler survey; among first to photograph Canyon de Chelly
Eadweard Muybridge returns to Sacramento to repeat "horse in motion" experiments; wins medal for landscape at Vienna International Exposition; photographs Modoc War
Carleton E. Watkins photographs in Utah with William Keith
Dr. Hermann Vogel discovers optical dye sensitizers, basis of orthochromatic photography

1874   William H. Jackson, with writer Ernest Ingersoll on Hayden survey, explores ruins of Mancos canyons; first to photograph dwellings there
John K. Hillers accompanies Powell on lecture tour, showing stereopticon slides
Carleton E. Watkins loses studio and gallery to creditors while away on photographic trip
Eadweard Muybridge jailed for murder of wife's lover
George Robertson spends two months in field recording Texas buffalo hunt
George Edward Anderson becomes apprentice in Charles Savage's "Pioneer Art Bazaar"

1875   William H. Jackson photographs in Southwest with Hayden survey, using 20-by-24-inch camera; writes "A Notice of the Ancient Ruins in Arizona and Utah Lying About the Rio San Juan," published by U.S. Geological Survey
John K. Hillers photographs Indian life in Oklahoma Territory for Powell
Timothy O'Sullivan spends final year with Wheeler survey; moves to Baltimore
Carleton E. Watkins creates "Watkins' New Series" to distinguish work from prints and negatives lost through debt
L. A. Huffman opens gallery in Iowa
Eadweard Muybridge acquitted of murder; photographs

landscape and journalistic subjects on trip to Central America; returns to San Francisco upon wife's death

1876 William H. Jackson organizes Department of Interior exhibit for Centennial Exposition in Philadelphia; compiles descriptive catalogue of extant photographs of North American Indians

Carleton E. Watkins makes mining and townscape views of Virginia City; begins to photograph California missions

Eadweard Muybridge continues "horse in motion" experiments; makes panoramas of San Francisco

National Photographic Association raises $20,000 by subscription to erect building for the display of photographs at Centennial Exposition, Philadelphia—exhibition signals highwater mark of collodion photography

1877 George Edward Anderson opens studio in Salt Lake City

William H. Jackson experiments unsuccessfully with new dry film from England

1878 Eadweard Muybridge, using twelve cameras, successfully photographs sequential motion of running horses at Stanford's Palo Alto Stock Farm; receives worldwide acclaim in scientific and artistic circles; applies for patent on "Method and Apparatus for Photographing Objects in Motion"; copyrights and publishes series of cards, "The Horse in Motion"

L. A. Huffman works in studio of F. J. Haynes; in September moves to Ft. Keogh, Montana Territory, to photograph military life

Albert Levy begins to produce dry plates for American market

1879 Timothy O'Sullivan obtains job as U.S. Geological Survey Bureau photographer under Director Clarence King

John K. Hillers photographs archaeological ruins in Arizona and New Mexico and disappearing tribal cultures of Pueblo Indians for Bureau of Ethnology, branch of Smithsonian Institution established by Powell

William H. Jackson ends government employ; opens Jackson Photographic Company in Denver

Eadweard Muybridge expands Palo Alto project with Stanford's backing, using twenty-four cameras

Camillus S. Fly arrives in Tombstone; travels through area

to photograph while wife maintains studio

George Edward Anderson, age nineteen, wins first place for tintype photography at Utah Territorial Fair

George Eastman begins to privately produce dry plates

1880 Timothy O'Sullivan begins work for U.S. Treasury Department

John K. Hillers's photographs used as basis for Clarence Dutton's "Report on the Geology of the High Plateaus of Utah"

Eadweard Muybridge terminates experimentation at Palo Alto; lectures and demonstrates "zoöpraxiscope," device which projects photographs on revolving disc, simulating motion

Carleton E. Watkins photographs trains, roundhouses, scenery along Southern Pacific Railroad, for Collis Huntington; photographs missions, Casa Grande; compiles portfolio of large views for Huntington

L. A. Huffman establishes gallery in Miles City, Montana; begins to photograph buffalo herds, cattlemen, and Indians; first to photograph Chief Two Moons, Cheyenne leader at Custer's Last Stand

Recognition of dry-plate process by Photographers' Association of America—beginning of modern "instantaneous" dry-plate photography (film has increased sensitivity, good shelf life, exposure time one-tenth to one-twentieth that of collodion)

George Eastman patents mechanical device to evenly coat emulsion on glass; begins commercial production of dry plates, distributed by E. & H. T. Anthony Company

1881 John K. Hillers placed in charge of U.S. Geological Survey photographic laboratory when Powell becomes director of consolidated bureau

William H. Jackson begins to make scenic and railway views for railroads

Eadweard Muybridge presents bound volume of 203 prints of subjects in motion to Stanford; journeys to Europe and advertises *The Attitudes of Animals in Motion*, offending Stanford by not acknowledging his support

L. A. Huffman photographs in Big Horn Mountains

George Edward Anderson establishes studio in Manti,

Utah, with partner L. D. Crandall

Patent issued to F. E. Ives for halftone process

"Cameras for the Millions" offered by E. & H. T. Anthony; competitive product from Scovill Manufacturing Company

1882   Eadweard Muybridge sues Stanford for publishing *The Horse in Motion* without giving him proper credit; lectures before elite societies including Royal Academy and Royal Geographical Society

George Hare introduces classic camera with baseboard and back hinged together; front standard capable of being set anywhere on movable board; widely copied

1883   William H. Jackson goes to Grand Canyon with Thomas Moran; makes first trip to Mexico

Solomon D. Butcher builds sod photographic studio in Custer County, Nebraska

George Eastman builds new factory for large-scale production of photographic materials

1884   Eadweard Muybridge accepts invitation to continue motion studies at University of Pennsylvania

Charles F. Lummis begins walk from Cincinnati to California

Eastman perfects process for making bromide-coated papers; patents an opaque, paper-based film; with William H. Walker, patents roll holder for film

Otto Schott develops barium crown glass—makes anastigmat lens possible

Dr. Hermann Vogel produces first orthochromatic negative emulsions

1886   Solomon D. Butcher begins work documenting land, history, and people of Custer County

Frederick I. Monsen accompanies U.S.-Mexican boundary survey; experiments with roll film

Camillus S. Fly accompanies Gen. George Crook to Sierra Mountains to photograph surrender of Geronimo; copyrights fifteen photographs from the series

Gelatin-bromide paper for printing produced in quantity by Eastman

Marked increase in halftone illustrations in magazines

1887   Eadweard Muybridge publishes *Animal Locomotion*, with

100,000 photographs, while working at University of Pennsylvania

John C. H. Grabill opens gallery in Sturgis, Dakota Territory

Hannibal Goodwin (original inventor of celluloid, flexible-base film) files for patent on film with transparent base

1888   Charles F. Lummis begins to make photographs; first known to photograph rites of Brothers of the Penitente

Eadweard Muybridge meets Thomas Edison to discuss combining Edison's "talking machine" with the zoöpraxiscope to "synchronously reproduce actions and words"

Eastman patents the Kodak, a camera with one speed, one fixed stop; makes one hundred circular pictures, 2 1/2 inches in diameter, utilizing stripping film on roll holder inside camera; film removed and processed by Eastman Kodak

John Carbutt devises cut film on celluloid, called "Carbutt's flexible negative film"

1889   A. A. Forbes photographs opening of Cherokee Strip in Oklahoma Territory; documents overnight rise of town

Eastman begins production of flexible-base nitrocellulose roll film (highly flammable)

Paul Rudolph develops anastigmat lens; manufactured by Carl Zeiss in 1890s

1890   Carleton E. Watkins, suffering ill health, makes last major trip to Pacific Northwest and British Columbia; photographs Anaconda Copper Mines in Montana

Frederick I. Monsen temporarily replaces injured Frank Nims as photographer on Brown-Stanton survey

C. P. Goerz markets camera with focal plane shutter in Germany

Halftone illustrations begin to appear in books

1891   Frederick I. Monsen unofficially joins Salton Sea expedition

John C. H. Grabill founds Portrait and View Company in Deadwood, Dakota Territory

Second generation of Kodaks, called ABC series, appears in December, featuring daylight loading and focusing adjustment; customer responsible for processing film

Bausch & Lomb patents pneumatic shutter

Thomas Edison and William Dickson invent the Kinetoscope, forerunner of motion-picture film and projector

1892 Adam C. Vroman goes West to settle in Pasadena, California
Charles F. Lummis photographs for a year in Bolivia and Peru with archaeologist Adolph Bandelier
C. P. Goerz manufactures double anastigmat lens
Thomas Ross Dallmeyer patents telephoto lens

1893 William H. Jackson appointed official photographer of World's Columbian Exposition in Chicago; prepares album of one hundred views
Eadweard Muybridge opens Zoöpraxographical Hall at World's Columbian Exposition; his forerunner of motion-picture projector eclipsed by Thomas Edison's Kinetoscope, which utilized long strips of perforated film
Frederick I. Monsen begins to lecture on Death Valley and desert areas
Patent issued to Louis and Max Levy for their process of halftone reproduction of illustrations (same process in use today)

1894 William H. Jackson publishes catalogue of panoramic views of Colorado and other landscapes; travels around world with World Transportation Commission
Eadweard Muybridge returns to England
Adam C. Vroman opens bookstore and first Kodak agency in southern California
Charles F. Lummis becomes editor of *Land of Sunshine*
George Edward Anderson builds two-story studio, G. E. Anderson Art Bazaar; travels around with portable studio to support gallery
Thomas Ross Dallmeyer introduces "Naturalist" camera, first to use true telephoto lens

1895 Adam C. Vroman makes first trip to photograph Hopi Snake Dance
Auguste and Louis Lumière in Paris demonstrate the Ciné-matographe, first motion-picture device, using sprocket-wound film (as in Edison's Kinetoscope) and projecting successive images on a screen
Focal plane shutters become commercially available in U.S.
Introduction of Pocket Kodak, first carriage-loading camera—forerunner of the Brownie produced in early 1900s
Penrose's Process begins annual publication

1896 Frederick I. Monsen works as artist and topographer on Yosemite National Park Survey; makes first trip to Southwest
Total sales of Kodak cameras surpass 100,000

1897 William H. Jackson becomes director, part-owner of Detroit Publishing Company, largest U.S. producer of photographic postcards
Adam C. Vroman travels to Enchanted Mesa, with Dr. Frederick W. Hodge, for Bureau of Ethnology
Frederick I. Monsen views Hopi Snake Dance for first time; meets Vroman there
George Edward Anderson photographs Mormon pioneers in Temple Square, Salt Lake City, to commemorate 50th anniversary of their arrival
Halftone illustrations become regular feature of newspapers
Folding pocket camera introduced; format becomes standard for years to come

1898 William H. Jackson makes photographs for commercial reproduction; begins to travel for Detroit Publishing Company to purchase local photographers' existing negatives
Adam C. Vroman forms small camera club for photographic excursions; privately publishes *Mission Memories*

1899 Solomon D. Butcher loses manuscript of Custer County history and many prints in fire; begins again to compile data and photographs
William H. Jackson visits Charles F. Lummis
Adam C. Vroman accompanies Dr. Frederick W. Hodge to photograph New Mexico pueblos; writes series of articles for *Photo-Era* magazine

1900 George Edward Anderson photographs Scofield mine disaster

1901 Solomon D. Butcher publishes *Pioneer History of Custer County*, containing two hundred photographic reproductions, in edition of one thousand

1902 William H. Jackson tours Southwest with display of Detroit Publishing Company work

1903 Adam C. Vroman makes last trip to Southwest

1905 Camillus S. Fly's wife publishes series of his photographs as *Scenes in Geronimo's Camp; the Apache Outlaw and Murderer* . . . .

1906 Carleton E. Watkins loses life's work in San Francisco earthquake and fire
Frederick I. Monsen loses many negatives and prints in San

Francisco holocaust; replaces some by copying selected works by Vroman

1907   Frederick I. Monsen begins lecturing and exhibiting photographs of Indian culture

George Edward Anderson appointed by Mormon church to undertake mission to England; begins photographic history of Mormon religion

Charles F. Lummis founds Southwest Museum in Highland Park, California

1909   A. A. Forbes moves to Bishop, California; becomes mining and commercial photographer

George Edward Anderson's photographs appear in *The Birth of Mormonism in Picture* by John Henry Evans, published by Deseret Sunday School Union, Salt Lake City

Frederick I. Monsen, accompanied by George Eastman, photographs in Southwest; trip results in booklet, *With A Kodak in the Land of the Navajo*, published by Eastman Kodak Co.

1920s   A. C. Hull's negatives destroyed by photographer renting his studio

1929   William H. Jackson publishes autobiography, *The Pioneer Photographer*

SELECTED BIBLIOGRAPHY

Works by Photographers of the West

Beaman, E. O. "The Cañon of the Colorado and the Moquis Pueblos"; "A Wild Boat-Ride Through the Cañons and Rapids"; "A Visit to the Seven Cities of the Desert"; "Glimpses of Mormon Life," *Appleton's Journal* 11 (April 18–May 30, 1874).

Bell, William A., papers. State Historical Society of Colorado, Denver.

———. *New Tracks in North America*, 2 vols. London: Chapman & Hall, 1869–70.

———. "Ten Days' Journey in Southern Arizona." In *Wonderful Adventures, A Series of Narratives of Personal Experiences Among the Native Tribes of America*. London: Cassell, Petter, Galpin & Co., 1872.

Butcher, Solomon. *Pioneer History of Custer County and Short Sketches of Early Days in Nebraska*. Broken Bow, Neb., 1901.

Carvalho, Solomon. *Incidents of Travel and Adventure in the Far West. . . .* New York: Derby & Jackson, 1857.

Curtis, Edward S. *In a Sacred Manner We Live*. Yonkers, N.Y.: World Book Co., 1915.

———. *In the Land of the Head-Hunters*. Yonkers, N.Y.: World Book Co., 1915.

———. *The North American Indian*. 20 vols. Cambridge, Mass.: The University Press, 1907–30.

———. "Vanishing Indian Types." *Scribner's Magazine* 39 (May, 1906; June, 1906).

Fly, C. S. *Scenes in Geronimo's Camp; the Apache Outlaw and Murderer. . . .* Tombstone, Ariz., 1905.

Forbes, A. A., family genealogy. University of Oklahoma Library, Norman. Western History Collections.

Gardner, Alexander. *Across the Continent on the Kansas Pacific Railroad—1867*. Missouri Historical Society, St. Louis.

———. *Gardner's Photographic Sketch Book of the War*. 2 vols. Washington, D.C.: Philip & Solomons, 1865–66.

———. *The John B. Sanborn Album*. Minnesota Historical Society, St. Paul. [original photographs]

Grinnell, George B. "Portraits of Indian Types." *Scribner's Magazine* 37 (March, 1905). [photographs by Edward S. Curtis]

Hayden, Ferdinand V. *Sun Pictures of Rocky Mountain Scenery, with a Description of the Geographical and Geological Features, and Some Account of the Resources of the Great West*. New York: J. Bien, 1870. [photographs by Andrew J. Russell]

Hillers, John K. *Pueblo Photographs of New Mexico*. Original photographs made for Dr. Frank Cushing. Huntington Library, San Marino, California.

Huntington Library, San Marino, California. Album 184. Stereographs of the Central Pacific Railroad. [includes photographs by Alfred A. Hart]

Jackson, William Henry. *Descriptive Catalogue of the Photographs of the United States Geological Survey of the Territories, for the Years 1869 to 1873, Inclusive*. n.p., 1869–73. Bancroft Library, University of California, Berkeley.

———. *The Diaries of William Henry Jackson, Frontier Photographer. . . .* Edited by Leroy R. Hafen and Ann W. Hafen. Glendale, Calif.: A. H. Clark, 1959.

———. "Field Work." *Philadelphia Photographer* 12 (1875).

———. *Photographs of Indians Selected from the Collection in the Possession of the U.S. Geological Survey of the Territories*. n.p., 1876. Yale University Library, New Haven, Connecticut. Western Americana Collection.

———. *Photographs of the Principal Points of Interest in Colorado, Wyoming, Utah, Idaho, and Montana, from Negatives Taken in 1869, '70, '71, '72, '73, '74, and '75. . . .* Washington, D.C.: Government Printing Office, 1876.

———. *Photographs of the Yellowstone National Park, and Views in Montana and Wyoming Territories*. Washington, D.C.: Government Printing Office, 1873.

———. *Time Exposure*. New York: G. P. Putnam's Sons, 1940.

———, and Driggs, Howard R. *The Pioneer Photographer*. Yonkers, N.Y.: World Book Co., 1929.

Lummis, Charles F. *General Crook and the Apache Wars*. Edited by Turbese Lummis Fiske. Flagstaff, Ariz.: Northland Press, 1969.

_____. "Hic Jacet Libbey." *Land of Sunshine* 7 (1897).

_____. *The Home of Ramona.* Los Angeles: C. F. Lummis & Co., 1888.

Monsen, Frederick I., papers. Huntington Library Archives, San Marino, California.

_____. "The Destruction of Our Indians." *Craftsman Magazine* 11 (1907).

_____. *Frederick Monsen Expeditions.* New York, 1913.

_____. *The Frederick Monsen Ethnographic Indian Photographs.* New York: Explorers Club, n.d.

_____. *With a Kodak in the Land of the Navajo.* Rochester, N.Y.: Eastman Kodak Co., n.d.

Moon, Carl, papers. Huntington Library Archives, San Marino, California.

_____. "American Indians of the Southwest." *Century Magazine* 74 (October, 1907).

Muybridge, Eadweard J. *Animal Locomotion. An Electro-Photographic Investigation of Consecutive Phases of Animal Movements. 1872–1885.* 11 vols. Philadelphia: University of Pennsylvania, 1887.

_____. Ibid., *Prospectus and Catalogue of Plates.* Philadelphia: University of Pennsylvania, 1887.

_____. *Animals in Motion: An Electro-Photographic Investigation of Consecutive Phases of Animal Progressive Movements.* London: Chapman & Hall, 1899.

_____. *Animals in Motion.* London: Chapman & Hall, 1901.

_____. *The Attitudes of Animals in Motion. A Series of Photographs Illustrating the Consecutive Positions Assumed by Animals in Performing Various Movements.* "Executed at Palo Alto, California, in 1878 and 1879, Copyright 1881, by Muybridge." Stanford University Libraries, Stanford, California. Rare Books and Special Collections.

_____. *Descriptive Zoöpraxography, or the Science of Animal Locomotion Made Popular.* Philadelphia: University of Pennsylvania, 1893.

_____. "A New Sky Shade." *Philadelphia Photographer* 5 (1869).

_____. *The Pacific Coast of Central America and Mexico; The Isthmus of Panama; Guatemala; and the Cultivation and Shipment of Coffee. Illustrated by Muybridge.* San Francisco, 1876. California State Library, Sacramento.

Palmer, W. J., and Bell, W. A. *The Development and Colonization of the "Great West."* London: Chapman & Hall, 1874.

Photographic Views of California Scenery. 112 of the Principal and Most Picturesque Places of California. 3 vols. Sacramento: State Office, 1886. California State Library, Sacramento.

Rankin, A. "He Knows the Redman." *Sunset* (February, 1920). [photographs by Carl Moon]

Russell, Andrew J. *The Great West Illustrated in a Series of Photographic Views Across the Continent: Taken Along the Line of the Union Pacific Railroad, West from Omaha, Nebraska*, vol. 1. New York, 1869.

_____. "A New Out-Door Camera Box." *Anthony's Photographic Bulletin* 1 (July, 1870).

_____. "On the Mountains with the Tripod and Camera." *Anthony's Photographic Bulletin* 1 (April, 1870; September, 1870).

_____. *Union Pacific Railroad Views, Across the Continent West from Omaha.* New York, 1869. [stereoscopic views]

Savage, Charles R. "A Photographic Tour of Near 9000 Miles." *Philadelphia Photographer* 4 (1867).

U.S. Geographical Surveys West of the 100th Meridian. *Photographs Showing Landscapes, Geological and Other Features, of Portions of the Western Territory of the United States, Obtained in Connection with Geographical and Geological Explorations and Surveys West of the 100th Meridian, Seasons of 1871, 1872, and 1873.* United States Geological Survey Library, Denver. [original photographs by Timothy O'Sullivan and William Bell]

Views of California. A Choice Collection of Photographic Views of the Yosemite Valley, Mammoth Trees, Transcontinental Railroad, Great Geyser Springs, Hydraulic and Placer Mining and San Francisco. San Francisco: Thomas Houseworth & Co., 1872.

Vroman, Adam Clark. Diary (Summer, 1895). Huntington Library, San Marino, California. Vroman Photographic Collection.

_____. Diary (Summer, 1897). Copy in William G. Webb Collection.

_____. *The Genesis of the Story of Ramona.* Los Angeles, 1899.

_____. "Katzimo, the Enchanted Mesa." *Photo-Era* 6 (1901).

_____. *Mission Memories.* Los Angeles, 1898.

Watkins, Carleton E., papers. Yosemite National Park Research Library, Yosemite, California.

_____. *Arizona and Views Adjacent to the Southern Pacific Railroad.* San Francisco, c. 1880.

_____. *Arizona and Views Adjacent to the Southern Pacific; Central Pacific Railroad and Views Adjacent.* 2 folio albums made for Collis

P. Huntington. Huntington Library, San Marino, California. [original photographs]

————. *New Almaden Quicksilver Mine*. San Francisco, n.d.

————. *Photographs of California and Oregon*. 2 folio albums. California State Library, Sacramento.

————. *Photographs of the Pacific Coast; Photographs of the Columbia River and Oregon;* and *Photographs of the Yosemite Valley*. 3 folio albums made for Mollie Latham. Stanford University Library, Stanford, California. Albert Bender Rare Book Room. [original photographs]

————. *Thurlow Lodge*. 2 folio albums made for Mollie Latham. San Mateo Historical Society, California. [original photographs]

————. *Yosemite Valley: Photographic Views of the Falls and Valley of Yosemite*. San Francisco, 1863.

Works on Photographers of the West

Akin, Louis. "Frederick Monsen of the Desert." *Craftsman* 11 (1907); 12 (1907).

Anderson, Ralph H. "Carleton E. Watkins, Pioneer Photographer of the Pacific Coast." *Yosemite Nature Notes* 32 (1953).

Andrews, Ralph W. *Curtis' Western Indians*. Seattle: Superior Pub. Co., 1962.

————. *Photographers of the Frontier West*. Seattle: Superior Pub. Co., 1965.

————. *Picture Gallery Pioneers*. Seattle: Superior Pub. Co., 1964.

Baumhofer, Hermine M. "T. H. O'Sullivan." *Image* 2 (April, 1953).

Belous, Russell E., and Weinstein, Robert A. *Will Soule: Indian Photographer at Fort Sill, Oklahoma, 1869–74*. Los Angeles: Ward Ritchie Press, 1969.

Brown, Joseph Epes, comp. "The North American Indians: A Selection of Photographs by Edward S. Curtis." *Aperture* 16, no. 4 (1972).

Brown, Mark H., and Felton, W. R. *Before Barbed Wire*. New York: Henry Holt and Co., 1956.

————. *The Frontier Years*. New York: Bramhall House, 1955.

Chrisman, Harry E. "The Sod House Photographs." *The West* 9 (1968).

Cunningham, Robert E. *Indian Territory*. Norman: University of Oklahoma Press, 1957.

Darrah, William C. "Beaman, Fennemore, Hillers, Dellenbaugh, Johnson and Hattan." *Utah Historical Quarterly* 16–17 (1948–49).

Daughters of the Utah Pioneers. "The Story of an Old Album." *Heart Throbs of the West* 9 (1948).

Dyck, Paul. *Sioux People of the Rosebud*. Flagstaff, Ariz.: Northland Press, 1971.

Eadweard Muybridge: The Stanford Years, 1872–1882. Stanford, Calif.: Stanford University Department of Art, 1972.

Fiske, Turbese Lummis, and Lummis, Keith. *Charles F. Lummis: The Man and His West*. Norman: University of Oklahoma Press, 1975.

Forsee, Aylesa. *William Henry Jackson, Pioneer Photographer of the West*. New York: Viking Press, 1964.

Francis, Rell G. "G. E. Anderson." *Popular Photography* 77 (1975).

Giffen, Helen S. "Carleton E. Watkins, California's Expeditionary Photographer." *Eye to Eye, Bulletin of the Graphic History Society of America* 6 (1954).

Gordon, Dudley. *Crusader in Corduroy*. Los Angeles: Cultural Assets Press, 1972.

Haas, Robert Bartlett. *Muybridge: Man in Motion*. Berkeley: University of California Press, 1975.

Haley, J. Evetts. *Focus on the Frontier*. Amarillo, Tex.: Shamrock Oil and Gas Corp., 1957.

Hall, Henry. "Restless, Troubled Opportunist: Portrait of a Pioneer Photographer." *Ramsey County History* 4 (1967).

Hendricks, Gordon. *The Photographs of Thomas Eakins*. New York: Grossman Publishers, 1972.

Hood, Mary V. "Charles L. Weed, Yosemite's First Photographer." *Yosemite Nature Notes* 38 (1959).

————, and Haas, Robert Bartlett. "Eadweard Muybridge's Yosemite Valley Photographs, 1867–1872." *California Historical Society Quarterly* 52 (March, 1963).

Horan, James D. *The Shadow Catcher*. New York: Crown Publishers, 1961.

————. *Timothy O'Sullivan: America's Forgotten Photographer*. Garden City, N.Y.: Doubleday & Co., Inc., 1966.

————. "Timothy O'Sullivan, Pioneer Photographer." *Westerner's Brand Book, New York Posse* 14 (1967).

————. "Timothy O'Sullivan, Pioneer Photographer of the West." *Westerner's Brand Book, New York Posse* 14 (1967).

Hurt, Wesley R., and Lass, William E. *Frontier Photographer: Stanley J. Morrow's Dakota Years*. Vermillion, S.D., and Lincoln, Neb.: University of South Dakota Press and University of Nebraska Press, 1956.

Jackson, Clarence S. *Picture Maker of the Old West*. New York: Charles Scribner's Sons, 1947.

Jerome, W. "Karl Moon's Indian Photographs." *Craftsman* 20 (1911).

Johnson, J. W. "The Early Pacific Coast Photographs of Carleton E. Watkins." *Water Resources Center Archives Series Report*, no. 8. Berkeley: University of California Press, 1960.

———. "Historical Photographs and the Coastal Engineer." *Shore and Beach* 29 (1961).

Lass, William E. "Stanley J. Morrow." *Eye to Eye, Bulletin of the Graphic History Society of America* 8 (1956).

Library of Congress. *Image of America: Early Photography, 1839–1900*. Washington, D.C., 1957.

MacDonnell, Kevin. *The Man Who Invented the Moving Picture*. Boston: Little, Brown and Co., 1972.

Mahood, Ruth I., ed. *Photographer of the Southwest: Adam Clark Vroman, 1856–1916*. Los Angeles: Ward Ritchie Press, 1961.

Mangan, Terry W. *Colorado on Glass*. Denver: Sundance Ltd., 1975.

Miller, Alan Clark. "Lorenzo Lorain, Pioneer Photographer of the Northwest." *American West* 9 (March, 1972).

Miller, Nina Hull. *Shutters West*. Denver: Sage Books, 1962.

Naef, Weston J., in collaboration with James N. Wood. *Era of Exploration: The Rise of Landscape Photography in the American West, 1860–1885*. Boston: New York Graphic Society, 1975.

Newhall, Beaumont, and Edkins, Diana E. *William H. Jackson*. Dobbs Ferry, N.Y.: Morgan & Morgan, for the Amon Carter Museum, 1974.

———, and Newhall, Nancy. *T. H. O'Sullivan: Photographer*. Rochester, N.Y.: George Eastman House, 1966.

New York Public Library. *Bulletin of the New York Public Library* 56 (1952).

Nitzsche, George E. "Pennsylvania Pioneering in the Movies." *General Magazine and Historical Chronicle*, Philadelphia: University of Pennsylvania 54 (1951).

Nye, Wilbur Sturtevant. *Plains Indian Raiders*. Norman: University of Oklahoma Press, 1968.

Pattison, William D. "The Pacific Railroad Rediscovered." *Geographical Review* 53 (1962).

———. "The Photographs of A. J. Russell." *American West* 6 (May, 1969).

Phillips, David R., comp. *The West: An American Experience*. Chicago: Henry Regnery, 1973.

Powell, Allan Kent. "Tragedy at Scofield." *Utah Historical Quarterly* 41 (Spring, 1973).

Powell, Lawrence Clark. "Photographer of the Southwest." *Westways* (August, 1958).

———. "A Southwest Bookseller." *Books: West Southwest; Essays on Writers, Their Books and Their Land*. Los Angeles: Ward Ritchie Press, 1957.

Rudisill, Richard, comp. *Photographers of the New Mexico Territory, 1854–1912*. Santa Fe: Museum of New Mexico, 1973.

Samson, John. "Photographs from the High Rockies." *Harper's New Monthly Magazine* 39 (September, 1869).

Schmitt, Martin F., and Brown, Dee. *Fighting Indians of the West*. New York: Charles Scribner's Sons, 1948.

Simpson, Jeffrey. *The Way Life Was*. New York: Praeger, 1974.

Steward, Julian H. "Notes on Hillers' Photographs of the Paiute and Ute Indians Taken on the Powell Expedition of 1873." *Smithsonian Miscellaneous Collections* 98 (1939).

Swanson, E. B. "Photographing the Grand Canyon Fifty Years Ago." *Mentor* 12 (1924).

Tilden, Freeman. *Following the Frontier with F. J. Haynes, Pioneer Photographer of the Old West*. New York: Alfred A. Knopf, 1964.

Turrill, Charles B. "An Early California Photographer: C. E. Watkins." *News Notes of California Libraries* 13 (1918).

Wadsworth, Nelson B. *Through Camera Eyes*. Provo, Utah: Brigham Young University Press, 1975.

———. "A Village Photographer's Dream." *Ensign* 3 (1973).

Watson, Elmo S. "Photographing the Frontier." *Chicago Westerner's Brand Book* 4 (1948).

———. "Shadow-Catchers of the Red Man." *Westerner's Brand Book, Denver Posse* 6 (1950).

———. "Way Out West." *Coronet* (April, 1939).

Webb, Walter Prescott. "A Texas Buffalo Hunt with Original Photographs." *Holland's Magazine* (1927).

Webb, William, and Weinstein, Robert A. *Dwellers at the Source:*

Southwestern Indian Photographs of A. C. Vroman, 1895–1904. New York: Grossman Publishers, 1973.

Wheelock, Walt. "Frémont's Lost Plates." *Westerner's Brand Book, San Diego Corral* 2 (1971).

White, John I. "Pages from a Nebraska Album." *American West* 12 (March, 1975).

Catalogues of Photographic Collections

A. A. Forbes Photographic Collection. A Descriptive List and Subject Index of Pictures. Norman: University of Oklahoma Library. Western History Collections.

Barry, David F. *Catalog of Photographs.* Denver Public Library. Western History Department.

"Catalog of Negatives, River, Land, and Ethnographic, 1871–1876." Washington, D.C.: Smithsonian Institution, National Anthropological Archives, mimeographed, n.d.

Chicago Photographers, 1847 through 1900. Chicago Historical Society, Print Department, 1958.

Faye, Helen, ed. *Picture Sources: An Introductory List.* New York: Special Libraries Association, 1959.

Mangan, Terry W. *Jackson's Colorado Negatives.* Denver: State Historical Society of Colorado.

Olivas, Arthur. *The Wittick Collection*, vol. 1. Santa Fe: Museum of New Mexico, 1971.

Rowbotham, Charles, and Mangan, Terry, docum. *Aultman Collection.* Denver: State Historical Society of Colorado, Resources Department, 1973.

Vanderbilt, Paul, comp. *Guide to the Special Collections of Prints and Photographs in the Library of Congress.* Washington, D.C.: Government Printing Office, 1955.

INDEX

PHOTOGRAPH LOANS

Note: Numbers refer to figures

The author and publisher wish to thank the following individuals, libraries, museums, and associations for permitting the reproduction of photographs in their collections. Their courtesy is gratefully acknowledged:

Amon Carter Museum of Western Art, Fort Worth: 28, 32, 38, 39, 44, 53, 57, 58, 60, 64; California State Library, Sacramento: 1, 2, 3, 11, 24, 25, 35, 56; Coffin's Old West Gallery, Miles City, Montana: 92, 93, 94, 98, 99, 101, 102, 103, 104; Barry Coombs, Union Pacific Rail Road: 66; Denver Public Library. Western History Collection: 15, 26, 27, 30, 41, 42, 43, 45, 47, 48, 49, 50, 51, 54, 56, 59, 61, 62, 65; Rell G. Francis, Heritage Prints, Springville, Utah: 107, 111, 113, 115, 116, 118, 119, 120, 121, 122, 123, 124, 127, 128; Huntington Library, San Marino, California: 4, 6, 7, 8, 10, 12, 13, 14, 18, 28, 67, 73, 74, 78, 86, 90, 91, 95, 152, 155, 156, 159, 160, 162, 163, 165, 166; Library of Congress, Washington, D.C.: 135, 137, 138, 139, 140, 141, 143, 144, 147; Glenn E. Miller, Lexington, Nebraska: 75, 77, 79, 80, 81, 82; Nebraska State Historical Society, Lincoln: 96, 97, 100, 105, 106, 108, 109, 110, 112; Pasadena Public Library, California: 148, 149, 150, 151, 153, 154, 157, 158; Smithsonian Institution National Anthropological Archives: 130, 132, 134, 136; Smithsonian Institution National Anthropological Archives, Bureau of American Ethnology Collection: 87, 89; Southwest Museum, Highland Park, Los Angeles: 142, 145, 146, 156; Stanford University Library, Stanford, California: 34, 36, 37, 40; State Historical Society of Colorado, Denver: 9, 16, 20, 21, 46, 63; Texas State Archives, Austin: 83, 84, 85, 88; University of Oklahoma Library, Norman. Western History Collections: 117, 125, 126, 129, 131, 133; U.S. Geological Survey: 5, 19, 22, 23, 31, 32; Utah Historical Society, Salt Lake City: 71, 76, 114; Yale University Library, New Haven, Connecticut. Western Americana Collection: 17, 52, 55, 68, 69, 70, 72, 110.